独墅湖畔 秀木成林
因聚而智 因融而能

Hi Five

西浦智能工程学院五周年纪念

[马来西亚] 林永义 编

苏州新闻出版集团
古吴轩出版社

图书在版编目（CIP）数据

独墅湖畔　秀木成林　因聚而智　因融而能 ：汉文、英文 / （马来）林永义编. -- 苏州 ：古吴轩出版社，2024. 9. -- ISBN 978-7-5546-2439-5

Ⅰ. G649.285.33

中国国家版本馆CIP数据核字第2024GC5127号

责任编辑： 俞　都

见习编辑： 王朝霞

装帧设计： 邹晓钢

书　　名： **独墅湖畔　秀木成林　因聚而智　因融而能**

编　　者： ［马来西亚］林永义

出版发行： 苏州新闻出版集团

古吴轩出版社

地址：苏州市八达街118号苏州新闻大厦30F

电话：0512-65233679　　　　邮编：215123

出 版 人： 王乐飞

印　　刷： 苏州市华方印务有限公司

开　　本： 889mm × 1194mm　1/16

印　　张： 7.75

字　　数： 156千字

版　　次： 2024年9月第1版

印　　次： 2024年9月第1次印刷

书　　号： ISBN 978-7-5546-2439-5

定　　价： 58.00元

HIVE

前言
FOREWORD

网络化、数字化、智能化（数智时代）正在重塑教育，加之多变的全球形势和复杂的社会背景，怎样变革和重塑教育，才能够培养驾驭人工智能等先进技术创造新生活和新世界、助力社会可持续发展的未来人才？

未来社会的人才需要强大的人机协作能力、沟通能力、自我管理能力及终身学习能力等行动力，需要国际视野、可持续发展意识、批判性思维、跨文化领导等思考模式，以“融合式智慧”直面未来的各种挑战。同时在 AGI 时代，人类很可能需要重新定位自己的社会价值甚至重新寻找生活的意义，此时心智模式起着关键作用。心智模式的不断升级和完善是人们更好地学习、成长、为人的基础，也是以人为本的未来教育的核心关注点。

The advent of networking, digitalisation, and intelligent technologies (the digitalisation and AI era) is reshaping education amidst a turbulent global environment and complex societal backdrop. How can we reform and reshape education to cultivate future talents capable of mastering advanced technologies like artificial intelligence, creating new worlds and lives, and contributing to sustainable societal development?

Future talents need strong capabilities in human-machine collaboration, communication, self-management, and lifelong learning. They require international perspectives, an awareness of sustainable development, critical thinking, and cross-cultural leadership to confront various future challenges with "syntegrative wisdom". In the era of AGI, humanity may need to redefine its social values and even seek new meanings in life, where mindset plays a crucial role. Continuous upgrading and refining of mindsets are foundational for better learning, growth, and humanity, and are the core focus of human-centred future education.

基于对未来人才需求的理解，西交利物浦大学（以下简称“西浦”）致力于营造跨越国界、跨越校园、需求导向、技术驱动的，重视个性化、兴趣导向、人机协作、融合式、终身学习、社会化的教育生态。

18 年来，西浦的未来教育理念在从“无”到“有”的实践和探索中不断完善和升级，我们的三种教育模式已逐渐被社会熟知。然而很多人会误解这三种教育模式是升级和迭代的关系，而事实上这是一个“三轨并行”的体系。人才是多维的、成功是多元的，三种教育模式从专业精英培养，到行业人才塑造，再到教育生态的创新，正是为支持学生个性化发展、满足面向未来的人才培养目标提供“有机”土壤，同时也为大学如何实现其服务社会的职能提供样板。

2019 年，西浦在 1.0 教育模式下将学院重组升级，旨在鼓励跨学科学习和合作，为师生提供既融合又开放的探索和创新平台。智能工程学院作为 1.0 模式下的旗舰学院之一，在成立 5 年以来，不但在其学科领域及跨学科创新教学、深耕科研，同时也主动引领三种教育模式之间的互动合作，助力产学研政社创新生态的搭建。

这本 5 周年纪念册，将带你浅阅我们智能工程学院成就背后的理念和故事，从不同视角感受一番西浦人在探寻未来教育道路上所作的努力和收获。让我们一起携手，回顾、反思过往，憧憬、擘画未来，面向新征程，再次出发！

席西民 教授

西交利物浦大学 执行校长

Understanding the needs of future talents, Xi'an Jiaotong-Liverpool University (hereafter referred to as "XJTLU") is committed to creating a borderless, campus-agnostic, demand-driven, technology-powered educational ecosystem. This ecosystem emphasizes personalized, interest-driven, human-machine collaborative, syntegrative, lifelong, and socialized learning.

Over the past 18 years, XJTLU's future education philosophy has evolved and improved through practical exploration from scratch. Our three educational models have become widely known in society. However, many people mistakenly believe these three models are iterative upgrades. In fact, they represent a "three-track parallel" system. Talents are multidimensional, and success is multifaceted. Our three educational models—from nurturing professional elites to shaping industry talents and leaders to innovating educational ecosystems—provide the "organic" soil for supporting personalized student development and meeting future talent cultivation goals. Simultaneously, they offer a blueprint for how universities can fulfill their social service functions.

In 2019, under the XJTLU 1.0 educational model, the restructuring and upgrading of schools aimed to encourage interdisciplinary learning and cooperation, providing an integrated and open platform for exploration and innovation for staff and students. The School of Advanced Technology, as one of the flagship schools of the 1.0 model, has not only innovated learning and teaching and deepened research within and across disciplines over the past 5 years but also actively led the interaction and cooperation among the three educational models, contributing to the construction of a university-industry-government-society innovation ecosystem.

This 5th-anniversary commemorative brochure will give you a glimpse into the concepts and stories behind the achievements of the School of Advanced Technology. From different perspectives, you will experience the efforts and gains of XJTLUers on the path of exploring future education. Let us join hands to review and reflect on the past, envision and plan for the future, and embark once again on a new journey towards the next level!

Professor Youmin Xi

Executive President, XJTLU

自 2019 年创立以来，智能工程学院就秉持其宏伟愿景，即在中国乃至全球范围内引领教学与科研、推动智能计算与工程技术的发展，并在相关先进技术领域占主导地位。在过去的五年里，学院始终以坚定不移的努力和奉献精神追求这一愿景。回顾这段旅程，可以清晰地看到，学院不仅实现了众多雄心勃勃的目标，更在多个领域实现了超越。如今，智能工程学院已经从最初的两个合并部门蜕变壮大，走出校园，发展成了一个集教学、科研和合作为一体的综合体。

在这本纪念册中，你将看到学院发展历程中的一系列显著成就和重要里程碑。我们的教师团队凭借深厚的专业知识与满腔热忱，持续投身于开拓性的科研项目。我们的学生和毕业生，在业界与先进技术领域内已树立起卓越的创业创新者形象，赢得了广泛赞誉。学院始终致力于构建充满协作精神与包容氛围的环境，让每一位学生和教职员工都能在这里尽情施展才华，充分释放潜能。

未来五年，智能工程学院将在其已建立的坚实基础上，探索技术领域的新高地，并继续营造教育卓越和科研革新的文化氛围。学院致力于引领尖端技术潮流，支持学生在日新月异的世界中出类拔萃。

这本纪念册向过去几年中为学院作出贡献的每一个人致敬，特别是我们敬业的教职员工、学生、校友和外部合作伙伴。你们的辛勤耕耘、非凡创造力和坚定支持，共同铸就了学院的辉煌成就。

我们诚挚地邀请你仔细研读本册中记载的每一个故事和成就，希望它们也能激发你的热情与梦想。智能工程学院已经谋划好未来，再次起航，期待你加入激动人心的发展新旅程。

致以美好的祝愿

阮周林 教授

西交利物浦大学 学术副校长

School of Advanced Technology was founded in 2019 with a visionary goal: to play a leading role in teaching and research in China and globally, in the development of intelligent computing and engineering, as well as associated fields of advanced technologies. The School has been pursuing this vision with unwavering effort and dedication over the past five years. Looking back on the journey, it is clear that the School has not only met but exceeded many of these ambitious aspirations. The School has now grown from two merged departments into a thriving unit of learning, teaching, research and industrial collaboration.

On these pages, you will find a series of remarkable achievements and significant milestones of the School. Our faculty, with their expertise and passion, have been undertaking ground-breaking research projects. Our students and graduates have established a strong reputation as entrepreneurial innovators in the industries and advanced technologies. The School's commitment to fostering a collaborative and inclusive environment has empowered students and staff to realise their full potential.

The next five years will see the School of Advanced Technology building on its solid foundation, exploring new frontiers in technology, and continuing to cultivate a culture of education excellence and research innovation. The School is committed to leading on the cutting edge technological advancements and supporting students to thrive in an ever-changing world.

This commemorative brochure is a tribute to everyone who has contributed to the success of the School over the past years, in particular, our dedicated faculty, staff, students, alumni, and external partners. Your hard work, creativity, and support have been instrumental in the School's achievements.

You are invited to delve into the stories and accomplishments captured in this brochure. May they inspire you as they have inspired us. The School of Advanced Technology is positioned for greater achievements in the years to come, and looking forward to your participation in the exciting journey ahead.

With best wishes

Professor Zhoulin Ruan

Vice President for Academic Affairs, XJTLU

目录 CONTENTS

院长手记
DEAN'S NOTE

学院的成立
THE FOUNDATION OF SAT

西浦是片充满活力与创新精神的土地，自成立之初就充满了对未来科技的无限憧憬。计算机科学与软件工程系及电气与电子工程系的并立，为后来智能工程学院的诞生奠定了坚实的基础。

随着岁月的流转，西浦如同一艘乘风破浪的巨轮，在知识的海洋中稳健前行。学生群体的日益壮大，教师团队的不断扩充与优化，如同汹涌的浪潮，推动着西浦向更高更远的目标迈进。面对这一蓬勃发展的态势，如何更有效地整合教学与科研资源，促进学科间的深度融合与交流，成了摆在所有西浦人面前的一项重要课题。

正是在这样的背景下，我们智能工程学院的诞生水到渠成。2019 年，一个崭新的里程碑在西浦的历史上被镌刻——智能工程学院正式成立，它不仅是西浦组织结构调整后建立的首个学院，更是西浦在培养未来科技领袖、推动跨学科融合方面迈出的重要一步。

The Department of Computer Science and Software Engineering and the Department of Electrical and Electronic Engineering were established with the founding of XJTLU. With the development of XJTLU and the increase in the number of students and teachers, to achieve integrated teaching and research resources for students and teachers, the two departments were merged and became the School of Advanced Technology in 2019. SAT is the pioneer school following the University academic strategy and restructure.

学院的成立，标志着原有的计算机科学与软件工程系、电气与电子工程系两大支柱院系完成了华丽的转身与重组。重组后的智能科学系、计算机系、电气与电子工程系、智能机电系和通信与网络工程系，共同驱动着智能工程学院这艘科技巨轮破浪前行。在这里，7 个本科专业、9 个硕士专业以及博士项目的全面覆盖，为学生搭建了从基础到前沿、从理论到实践的全方位学习平台。

智能工程学院的建立，不仅仅是学科布局的优化调整，更是教育理念与模式的一次深刻变革。学院致力于打破传统学科的壁垒，鼓励跨学科研究与教学，为师生创造了一个自由开放、充满挑战与机遇的学术环境。在这里，教师们能够依托更加完善的科研设施与教学资源，深耕细作，探索未知；学生们则能在挑战中成长，在合作中进步，逐步成长为既精通专业知识，又具备卓越沟通能力、团队合作精神及项目管理能力的复合型人才。

The School of Advanced Technology constitutes 5 departments which have complementary skills that are in demand worldwide:Department of Intelligent Science (INT), Department of Computing (CPT), Department of Electrical and Electronic Engineering (EEE), Department of Mechatronics and Robotics (MEC), Department of Communications and Networking (CAN). SAT hosts 7 Undergraduate programmes, and 9 Postgraduate programmes each served by the 5 departments. Meanwhile, the school also operates highly successful research-based Doctoral programmes.

The School facilitates resource concentration and management including administrative and technical personnel to support Departments, and encourages interdisciplinary academic activities and outreach. This new family has created an innovative teaching and research resources for our staff, and provided our students with a challenging and stimulating environment to unlock their full potential.

江苏省工程研究中心建设

JIANGSU ENGINEERING RESEARCH CENTER

时光荏苒，转眼来到了 2020 年 11 月。科研办公室的一则通知，犹如一声号角，吹响了 2020 年江苏省工程研究中心申报的集结号。此时距离递交材料的截止日期仅有不足一周的时间，时间紧迫，任务艰巨。面对这样的挑战，我和我的团队没有丝毫退缩，我们毅然决然地投入到这场与时间赛跑的战斗中。

Time has flown by, and all of a sudden it's November 2020. A notification from the Research Office issued a rallying call for the 2020 Jiangsu Engineering Research Center application, much like a call to arms. With just under a week left until the submission deadline, time was of the essence and the task loomed large. In the face of this challenge, neither I nor my team hesitated, and we wholeheartedly threw ourselves into this race against time.

我们申报的省工程研究中心，是以西浦人工智能产业研究院为基石而建立的。这座平台已历经三年的沉淀，汇聚了西浦 21 名人工智能领域的专家学者，他们的智慧与汗水共同铸就了今天的辉煌。尽管我们在人工智能领域已积累了一定的经验，但面对首次代表学校申请省级科研平台建设项目这一重任，我心中仍不免忐忑。

The Jiangsu Province Engineering Centre we were about to apply for was founded on the grounds of the Xi'an Jiaotong-Liverpool University Artificial Intelligence University Research Centre (XJTLU AI-URC) . This platform, developed over three years, has brought together 21 experts and scholars in the field of artificial intelligence, whose wisdom and hard work have collectively contributed to today's success. While we had garnered some experience in the field of artificial intelligence, the responsibility of representing the university to apply for a provincial scientific research platform construction project for the first time left me feeling somewhat anxious.

与此同时，我们深知竞争之激烈。省内各大高校、科研院所都在积极备战，他们的实力不容小觑。然而，我和我的团队并没有因此而气馁。我们深知，只有立足当下、齐心协力，才能在这场竞争中脱颖而出。于是，我们开始了夜以继日的努力。

At the same time, we were acutely aware of the fierce competition. Major universities and research institutes in the province were actively gearing up, and their capabilities were not to be underestimated. However, neither I nor my team were disheartened by this reality. We recognized that only by pooling our efforts and staying rooted in the present could we stand out in this competition. Therefore, we began to exert tireless efforts day and night.

申请材料的撰写与修改，成了我们每天的主要工作。我们不断地查阅资料、梳理数据、分析成果，力求将最全面、最前沿、最权威的报告呈现给评审专家。每一次的修改，都是对细节的极致追求；每一次的沟通，都是对团队精神的磨砺。我们已记不清申请材料修改了多少个版本，组内沟通会议开了多少次，但我们始终坚守着初心，用汗水和智慧书写着属于我们的篇章。

The drafting and revising of application materials became our primary daily task. We consistently referred to materials, organized data, and analyzed results, aiming to present the most comprehensive, cutting-edge, and authoritative report to the review experts. Each revision was an exacting pursuit of detail, and each communication was a tempering of team spirit. We couldn't recall how many versions of the application materials we had revised or how many internal communication meetings we had conducted, but we unwaveringly held onto our initial aspirations, recording our story with perseverance and sagacity.

在学校各个部门的鼎力支持下，我们终于在 2020 年 12 月底迎来了喜讯——我们成功获得了江苏省工程研究中心的荣誉称号。这一刻，所有的付出与努力都得到了回报。这份荣誉不仅是对我们科研成果的肯定，更是对我们团队精神的赞誉。

站在新的起点上，我们将不忘初心、砥砺前行。我们将继续深耕人工智能领域，为推动科技进步和社会发展贡献我们的智慧和力量。我们相信，在未来的日子里，我们将书写更多属于西浦人工智能产业研究院的辉煌篇章！

With comprehensive support from various departments in the University, we finally received good news at the end of December 2020—we successfully secured the accolade of the Provincial Engineering Research Center. At that moment, all our endeavors and hard work bore fruit. This honor not only validated our research accomplishments but also commended the spirit of our team.

Standing at a new starting point, we will not forget our original intentions and will continue to delve into the field of artificial intelligence, contributing our wisdom and strength to drive technological progress and societal development. We believe that in the days ahead, we will carve out more brilliant chapters for the XJTLU AI-URC.

学院获得的认可
RECOGNITION OF THE SCHOOL

我们拥有一个结构合理且兼具国际化背景、前沿学科科研能力和丰富教学经验的高水平学术团队。学院的教师们不仅是学术研究的佼佼者，更是学生成长道路上的引路人。他们积极参与国内外各类科研活动，频频在计算机科学、工程科学等多个领域获得高度评价与认可，其卓越的科研能力不仅为学生提供了最前沿的知识与技术支持，更激发了学生们对科学探索的无限热情与好奇心。在这样的学术氛围下，学生们得以在科研的海洋中自由遨游，不断挑战自我，实现个人潜能的最大化。

SAT has a well-structured, high-level academic team with diverse international backgrounds, cutting-edge scientific research ability and rich teaching experience. Our academics actively participate in cutting-edge research and are internationally recognized in many fields. Their excellent academic abilities ensures that students receive professional support and guidance, engendering a school grounded in professionalism and innovation.

2021 年泰晤士高等教育世界大学学科排名中，西交利物浦大学计算机科学与社会科学学科位于全球 201—250 名区间，工程学位于全球 251—300 名区间，我们智能工程学院所有专业均属其中。也是在 2021 年，全校共有两个学科进入 ESI 大学排行榜的全球前 1%，分别是工程科学和计算机科学，涵盖智能工程学院的所有研究领域。排名的提升意味着西浦的相关学科发表论文的被引用量达到了全球前 1%，是高质量教研的真实反映。

XJTLU is currently ranked 201-250 for computer science, 251-300 for engineering in the Times Higher Education (THE) World Subject Rankings 2021. All of SAT's academic offerings are included within these two fields.Engineering and Computer Science in XJTLU was ranked in the ESI's top 1% in 2021. It is a significant achievement of the whole school and a genuine reflection of the quality of the research and research-led teaching delivered by SAT.

尤为值得一提的是，我们学院在国际认证方面也取得了显著成就。数字媒体技术、通信工程、电气工程及其自动化、电子科学与技术等多个本科专业以及硕士专业均获得了英国工程技术协会（IET）的认证。计算机科学与技术、信息与计算科学、数字媒体技术、应用信息学、社会网络计算技术、计算机科学、模式识别与智能系统（研究型）等多个本科专业以及硕士专业均获得英国计算机协会（BCS）认证，除了近几年新开设的专业，学院所有工程类及计算机科学类专业均已获得国际认证。

BEng Digital Media Technology, BEng Communication Engineering, BEng Electrical Engineering, BEng Electronic Science and Technology undergraduate programmes and three master's programmes have been accredited by the UK's Institute of Engineering and Technology (IET). BEng Computer Science and Technology, BSc Information and Computer Science, and BEng Digital Media and Technology, and four master's programs have been accredited by the British Computer Society (BCS). Except for the newly opened programmes in recent years,all engineering and computer science programmes of the school have obtained international professional accreditation.

IET The Institution of Engineering and Technology

bcs Accredited Degree

此外，在江苏省教育厅公布的“十四五”省重点学科名单中，智能工程学院的计算机科学与技术学科再次脱颖而出，成功入选江苏省重点学科。这一荣誉不仅彰显了学院在学科建设方面的卓越成就，更为学院未来的发展奠定了坚实的基础。

凭借优秀的学术团队、卓越的科研能力、广泛的国际影响力以及不断攀升的学科实力，我们学院获得了越来越多的国际认可，也为学生的未来发展提供了更加广阔的空间与机遇。

The Computer Science and Technology discipline from the School of Advanced Technology at XJTLU won the 14th Five-year Jiangsu Key Discipline Award, the second time this discipline has received such an award, after also obtaining the 13th Five-Year Jiangsu Key Discipline Award and successfully passing the final acceptance check.

As a young school, School of Advanced Technology has improved its teaching and research quality year by year and has obtained ever increasing international recognition for its academic activities.

小红书大冒险
ADVENTURE ON RED

2022 年，对于学院来说，是充满探索与尝试的一年，我们正式开通了智能工程学院官方小红书账号——小智大能，自此踏上视频创作的“新赛道”。

小红书这个在年轻人中广受欢迎的社交平台，以其独特的视觉呈现和活跃的社区氛围，吸引了我们的目光。我们意识到，科学技术的内容有时难以通过文字全面展现，而小红书以图片、视频为主的传播方式，为我们提供了将复杂的科技知识变得直观、生动的可能。

In 2022, our school embarked on a year of exploration and experimentation as we officially launched the School of Advanced Technology account—Xiao Zhi Da Neng, on RED, marking the beginning of a new journey in video creation.

RED, a popular social media platform among young people, has captivated us with its unique visual presentation and vibrant community atmosphere. Recognizing that scientific and technological content can sometimes be challenging to express fully through text, we appreciate how RED's primarily image- and video-based communication style allows us to make complex technological knowledge more intuitive and vivid.

开设小红书账号的初衷，是希望拉近师生距离，并且向更多的在校学生、潜在学生、家长以及对科技充满好奇的人群，展现西浦智能工程学院活泼、创新的一面。为此，我们制订了详细的运营计划，确保每周更新内容，保持与粉丝的互动与交流。在内容策划上，我们采取“硬植入”与“软植入”相结合的方式。

The primary goal behind creating the RED account was to bridge the gap between teachers and students and to showcase the lively and innovative side of the School of Advanced Technology to current and prospective students, parents, and those curious about technology. We have developed a detailed operating plan to ensure weekly updates and maintain interaction and communication with our followers to achieve this.

一方面，我们会定期分享最新的学院专业信息、师资介绍、毕业数据等内容，让外界更全面地了解西浦、了解智能工程学院，为我们的招生、科研及行业合作提供助力；另一方面，我们鼓励学院师生多多参与拍摄，通过各种有趣的学院活动、科普内容、游戏挑战等，让大家感受到学院的活力与魅力。

Regarding content planning, we have adopted direct and indirect approaches. On the one hand, we regularly share the latest information about the school's programmes, faculty introductions, graduation statistics, and other content to provide a comprehensive understanding of XJTLU and our school, supporting our enrollment, scientific research, and industry cooperation. On the other hand, we invite the school students and faculty to join the filming to showcase the school's vitality and charm through various exciting activities, science popularization content, game challenges, and more.

比如，在 2022 年开学季，我们尝试推出了一期校园探索视频，带即将入学的新生们“游玩”几个西浦地标，并率先参与到大学的探楼视频拍摄中，去了毕业生们都非常惦念的基础楼和工科楼。

For example, during the 2022 academic year's opening season, we released a campus tour video, guiding incoming first-year students to visit several landmarks of XJTLU. We also pioneered filming university building tour videos, allowing graduates to revisit the much-missed Foundation Building and Engineering Building.

小红书“小智大能”这个全新的展示窗口是我们与粉丝互动、分享学院精彩瞬间的乐园。在这里，我们将不断探索和创新，让学院的风采展示更加丰富、多元。期待每一位关注我们的粉丝，都能在这里找到属于自己的乐趣。

Xiao Zhi Da Neng, this brand-new showcase, has become a paradise for us to interact with our followers and share the exciting moments of the school. Here, we will continue to explore and innovate, delving into diverse and attractive topics. I hope every follower can find their own joy here!

西浦一百度人工智能创新联合体的诞生

UNVEILING THE XJTLU-BAIDU AI INNOVATION ALLIANCE

2023 年 9 月 2 日，经过近一年的筹备和努力，由智能工程学院参与建设的西浦一百度人工智能创新联合体（以下简称“创新联合体”）终于正式揭牌了。这个由苏州工业园区管委会、西交利物浦大学和百度集团联合共建的项目，翻开了数智化时代下，政府、高校、企业在科技领域携手合作，共谋发展的新篇章。

在筹备期间，我们经历了无数次的会议、讨论和提案修改。每一次讨论都让我们更加坚定了我们的方向。构建一个“教育、科技、人才”三位一体的创新生态平台不仅仅是一个口号，更是我们实实在在的行动。它不仅包括一个西交利物浦大学一人工智能学院，还设立了百度智能云千帆大模型平台（苏州）创新中心和百度智能云数智能碳（苏州）赋能中心。每一个子项目都承载着我们对未来教育和产业发展的美好愿景。

The XJTLU-Baidu Artificial Intelligence Innovation Alliance, the first of its kind in China, was officially launched on September 2nd, 2023, to support the development of an open, world-class high-tech ecosystem in Suzhou and beyond.The alliance is a partnership of Xi'an Jiaotong-Liverpool University, technology giant Baidu, and Suzhou Industrial Park. The School of Advanced Technology has also played a key role in its establishment.

We engaged in countless meetings, discussions, and proposal revisions throughout the preparation period. Each discussion served to strengthen our determination and clarify our direction.

The alliance consists of three main units: the XJTLU Academy of AI will cultivate high-level professionals; the Baidu AI Cloud Qianfan Large Scale Model Platform Innovation Centre will explore large-scale model technology research; and the Baidu AI Cloud Smart Carbon (Suzhou) Empowerment Centre will focus on energy, biological medicine, and smart city development. Each unit carries our vision for the future of education and industry development.

西浦是一所敢于创新的年轻大学，在不同发展阶段有针对性地采取不同的教育模式和发展战略。目前，我们正在积极建设西交利物浦大学—人工智能学院，这是大学教育改革和创新的重要一步。我们非常荣幸能够参与其中，打造又一个西浦 3.0 学院，发挥黏合剂和发酵剂作用，撬动各方资源，营造教育、研究、创新、创业的产业生态。

我们引入了国内顶级的全栈 AI 技术，将底层技术、工程工具和实际产业应用案例与产业岗位需求相结合，充分利用西浦智能工程学院师资队伍优势和现有的硕士专业基础，开发 AI+ 课程；同时，我们也在积极探索人工智能多学科的交叉融合，以及“人工智能 + X”复合专业人才培养的新模式，以期培养出具有国际视野、创新精神和实践能力的人才，助力科技进步和产业升级。

我们希望通过这种跨学科的教育模式，让学生能够在学习中直接接触到最前沿的技术和应用，为未来职业生涯打下坚实的基础。

We are currently actively building the XJTLU Academy of AI , an important step in our university's educational reform and innovation. As a young university with a spirit of innovation, XJTLU adopts different educational models and development strategies at various stages of its growth. We are honoured to be part of building this academy as another XJTLU 3.0 project and leveraging our unique position to serve as a bonding agent, catalyst, and booster to promote the integration of academia, industry, government, and society.

We have introduced top-notch full-stack AI technology in China, combining underlying technology, engineering tools, and real-world industrial cases to meet the needs of the industry. We are developing AI+ courses based on the XJTLU School of Advanced Technology faculty team and the existing master's professional foundation. Simultaneously, we are actively exploring the cross-disciplinary integration of AI and the “AI + X” method to train versatile professionals.

We hope this interdisciplinary education model can give our students direct access to the most cutting-edge technology and applications in their studies, laying a solid foundation for their future careers. We can also cultivate talents with an international perspective, innovative spirit, and practical ability, contributing to technological progress and industrial upgrading.

学者的跨界之旅
TRAILBLAZING BEYOND THE CAMPUS

2024 年 5 月 18 日，我参与录制的《城市课堂》节目正式播出了。节目里，我和一群活泼可爱的初高中学生们面对面交流，探讨了我们共同关心的话题：人工智能。看着他们好奇的样子，听着他们充满想象力的提问，我愈发感受到传播科学知识的意义。

On May 18, 2024, the *City Lecture* program I participated in was officially broadcast. During the event, I engaged in direct discussions with a group of delightful middle and high school students, delving into a topic we all cared about:artificial intelligence. Witnessing their curious expressions and fielding their imaginative questions only reinforced my belief that disseminating scientific knowledge is a meaningful thing to do.

我们身处科技前沿，近五年来，学院越来越多的老师开始走出校园，参与到各种社会话题的讨论中，在学术领域深耕细作的同时，也在社会舞台上发出自己的声音，肩负起一份社会责任。他们基于自己的研究领域，对一些行业问题进行评价和讨论。比如，当 ChatGPT 这样的新技术出现时，我们学院的老师们积极探讨它对高校教育、学生发展以及教师角色的影响。

We stand at the forefront of technology. Over the past five years, more and more academics in our school have begun to step out of the campus and participate in discussions on various social topics. While immersing themselves in their academic pursuits, they also voice their opinions on the social stage and shoulder this social responsibility. They evaluate and discuss industries based on their areas of research. For example, with the emergence of new technologies like ChatGPT, our school's academics actively explore AI's impact on higher education, student development, and the role of teachers.

如果能够通过这样的方式，为社会带来一些有价值的思考，激发更多人对科技的兴趣，引导社会大众对科技的正确理解和使用，那就太好了！

If we can bring some valuable thinking to society through such efforts, inspire more people's interest in science and technology, and steer the correct understanding and use of technology, that would be great!

此外，在西浦最近公布的学术卓越奖名单上，共有 8 位学者凭借他们的学术成果、教学能力获奖，其中 5 位都来自智能工程学院。

Additionally, in the recently released university announcement of AY2023-2024 XJTLU Academic Excellence Awards, a total of 8 faculty members have received Prize for their outstanding academic accomplishments and teaching abilities. Notably, 5 of these awardees are from the School of Advanced Technology.

能够带领这样一个充满活力和责任感的优秀团队，我真的深感荣幸。

I am truly honoured to lead such an excellent, dynamic, and responsible team.

2022.1“计算机科学与技术”学科成功入选“十四五”江苏省重点建设学科

2022.1 Computer Science and Technology was selected for the Jiangsu 14th 5-year Key Discipline

2022.3.29 三个本科专业及四个硕士专业荣获英国计算机学会（BCS）认证

2022.3.29 Three undergraduate programmes and four postgraduate programmes obtained accreditation from the British Computer Society (BCS)

2022.8.16 学院入选中国半导体行业协会集成电路分会人才储备基地

2022.8.16 SAT was selected as a talent reserve base for the Integrated Circuit Branch of China Semiconductor Industry Association

2022.8.23“电气工程及其自动化”专业入选江苏高校品牌专业建设工程二期项目（省特色专业）

2022.8.23 Electrical Engineering was selected for the second phase of the Jiangsu University Brand Programme Construction Project (Provincial Characteristic Programme)

2022.9.21 第一届西浦智能工程学院科研与产业日

2022.9.21 The first SAT Research and Industry Day

2021.4 新硕士专业——人机交互硕士获批

2021.4 New Master's programme—Msc Human-Computer Interaction approved

2021.6 “计算机科学与技术”学科圆满完成“十三五”江苏省重点建设学科终期验收

2021.6 Computer Science and Technology successfully completed the final acceptance of Jiangsu 13th 5-year key discipline construction

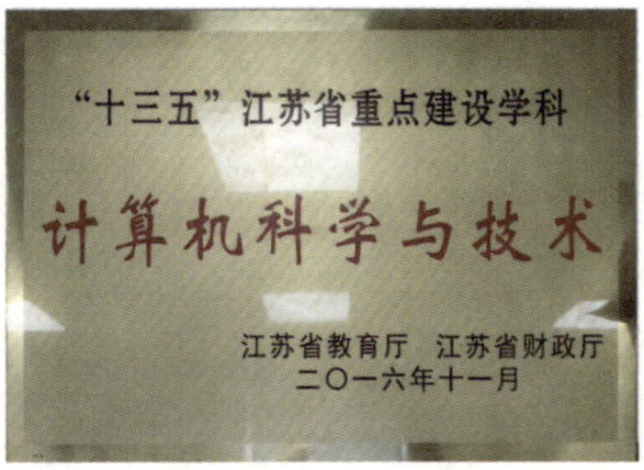

2021.7.11 西交利物浦大学计算机科学领域首次进入ESI全球前1%

2021.7.11 Entered the ESI Top 1% list of institutions in the field of Computer Science for the first time

2021.7.28 第一届SAT工业咨询委员会会议

2021.7.28 First Meeting of SAT Industrial Advisory Board

2021.12 余凌云、王璟琛2人获江苏省人才项目，靳小波获评江苏省“青蓝工程”中青年学术带头人，杨瑞获评江苏省“青蓝工程”优秀青年骨干，肖继民、王秋锋2人获评江苏省“333工程”第三层次人才，王新珩获评独墅湖科教创新区国际型学科领军人才，林永义、孙捷、朱晓辉、张杰、宋鹏飞5人获评独墅湖科教创新区科教骨干人才

2021.12 Lingyun Yu and Jingchen Wang awarded Jiangsu talent project; Xiaobo Jin and Rui Yang awarded Jiangsu Qinglan talent; Jimin Xiao and Qiufeng Wang awarded Jiangsu 333 Engineering Project talent; Xinheng Wang, Eng Gee Lim, Jie Sun, Xiaohui Zhu, Jie Zhang and Pengfei Song awarded SIP SEID key talent

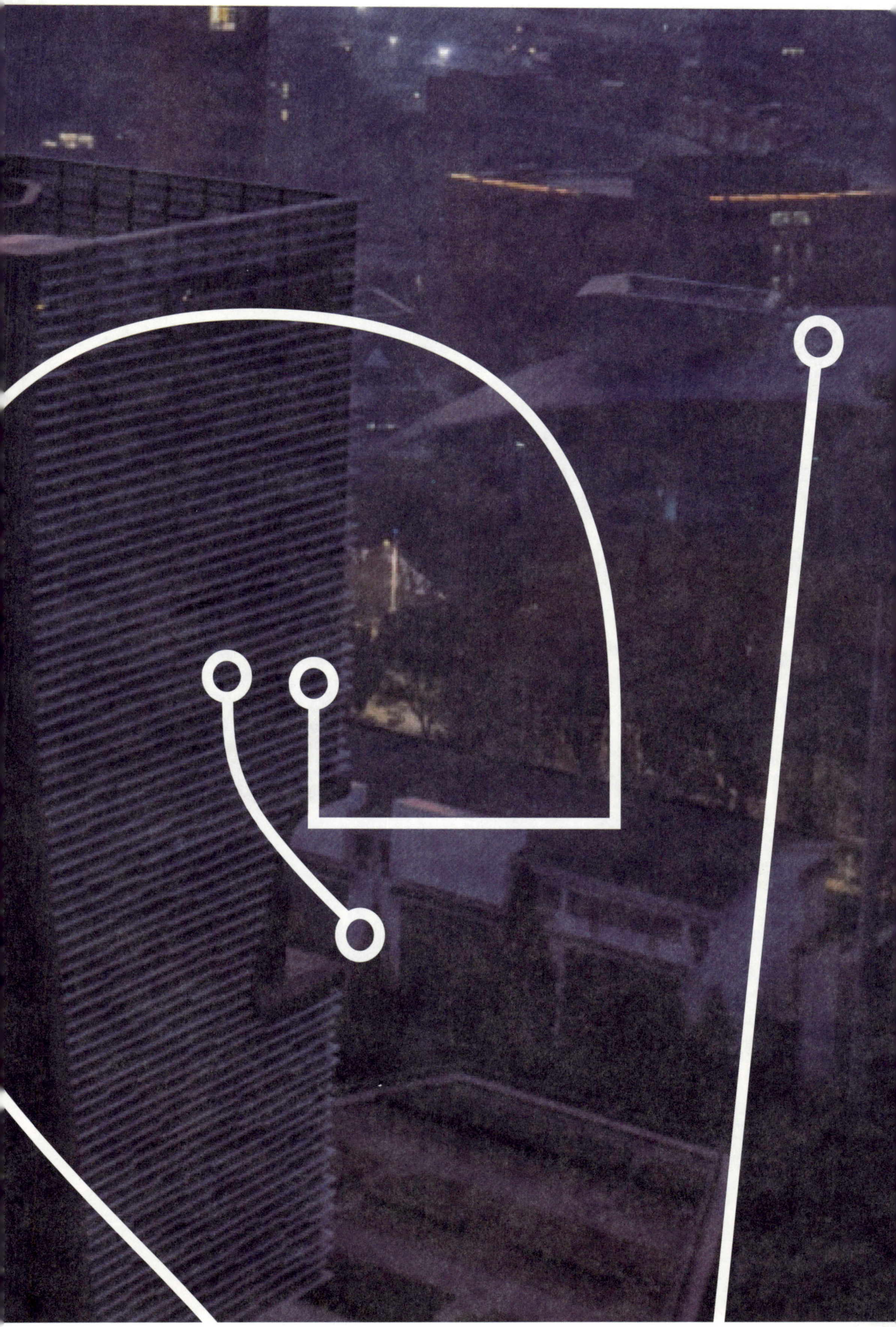

2019.9.1 融合两个系，智能工程学院正式成立

2019.9.1 School of Advanced Technology established through the extraordinary merger of the two Departments-Computer Science and Software Engineering & Electrical and Electronic Engineering

2020.1 新硕士专业——模式识别和智能系统（研究型硕士）获批

2020.1 New Master's programme—MRes Pattern Recognition and Intelligent Systems approved

2020.7.11 西交利物浦大学工程领域首次进入ESI全球前1%

2020.7.11 Entered the Essential Science Indicators Top 1% list of institutions in the field of Engineering for the first time

2020.9 学院三门计算机及数据类课程获“十三五”江苏高校外国留学生英文授课精品课程

2020.9 Three computer and data modules awarded the 13th 5-year English-taught elite courses in Jiangsu universities

2019.12 刘庆获评江苏省人才项目，马洁明获评江苏省“青蓝工程”优秀青年骨干，宋鹏飞、杨瑞、陈建军3人获评苏州工业园区高层次和紧缺人才薪酬补贴

2019.12 Qing Liu awarded Jiangsu talent project; Jieming Ma awarded Jiangsu Qinglan talent; Pengfei Song, Rui Yang and Jianjun Chen awarded SIP talent subsidy

2020.12 西交利物浦大学获评苏州市人工智能学会理事会长单位

2020.12 XJTLU awarded Chairman Unit of Suzhou Artificial Intelligence Society

2020.12 陈建军、宋鹏飞、杨瑞、杨曦4人获江苏省人才项目，张杰获苏州工业园区高层次和紧缺人才薪酬补贴，王炤、陈敏、肖继民、孙捷、王秋锋5人获评独墅湖科教创新区科教骨干人才

2020.12 Jianjun Chen, Pengfei Song, Rui Yang and Xi Yang awarded Jiangsu talent project; Jie Zhang awarded SIP talent subsidy; Zhao Wang, Min Chen, Jimin Xiao, Jie Sun and Qiufeng Wang awarded SIP SEID key talent

问道：学院成长之路

THE JOURNEY OF SCHOOL GROWTH

求真：
科研创新之旅

THE JOURNEY OF RESEARCH INNOVATION

2024.2 目前学院共获批5项教育部产学合作协同育人项目

2024.2 Five Industry—University Cooperation and Education Projects approved by the Ministry of Education

2024.5 学院成功举办“慧聚独墅湖 × 创新活力秀”校企合作交流会西浦智能工程学院—人工智能领域专场

2024.5 SAT successfully held the "Wisdom Gathering at Dushu Lake × Innovation and Vitality Show" school—enterprise cooperation exchange meeting: XJTLU School of Advanced Technology- artificial intelligence special session

2024

2024.6.1 学院在籍学生规模达3881人，其中本科生3406人，硕士生248人，博士生227人

2024.6.1 SAT currently has 3881 registered students, including 3406 UG students, 248 PG students and 227 PhD students

2024.6 526名本科生参与116项暑期本科生科研项目，创历史新高

2024.6 526 UG students engaged in 116 SURF projects, hitting new record high

2024.6 省级以上学生竞赛获奖累计超过500人次

2024.6 Over 500 students won awards in provincial, national and international student competitions

2024.7 学院专任教师人数达到100人，英国高等教育学会会士人数达38人

2024.7 The number of SAT academic staff reached 100, 38 academic staff achieved FHEA

2024.7 SAT“探索与引领”系列学术报告已成功举办22期

2024.7 SAT "Exploring and Leading" academic seminar series have been successfully held for 22 sessions

2024.9.1 学院成立五周年

2024.9.1 SAT 5th anniversary

2023.8.18 本科生团队连续三年进军RoboMaster机甲大师全国决赛，获1个一等奖及2个二等奖

2023.8.18 UG student teams won in RoboMaster national competition for the past three consecutive years, awarded 1 first prize and 2 second prizes

2023.8.25 本科学生团队获第六届全国大学生智能机器人创新大赛一等奖

2023.8.25 UG Student teams received first prize in China's 6th National University Contest on Intelligent Robotic Innovations

2023.12 季成涛、许旭、石英力、潘昱杉4人获评江苏省人才项目，马洁明获评江苏省“青蓝工程”中青年学术带头人，武芳宇获评姑苏领军青年创新人才，赵春获评苏州市优秀教育工作者，王秋锋、肖继民、李圣辰、岳勇、俞凌云、马洁明、张杰7人获评独墅湖科教创新区科教骨干人才，陈晓阳、赵春2人获评独墅湖科教创新区校企导师互聘访问工程师教师

2023.12 Chengtao Ji, Xu Xu, Yingli Shi and Yushan Pan awarded Jiangsu talent project; Jieming Ma awarded Qinglan talent;Fangyu Wu awarded Gusu leading talent; Chun Zhao awarded Suzhou outstanding educator; Qiufeng Wang, Jimin Xiao, Shengchen Li, Yong Yue, Lingyun Yu, Jieming Ma and Jie Zhang awarded SIP SEID key talent; Xiaoyang Chen and Chun Zhao awarded SIP SEID visiting engineer teacher

2019.10.25 杨曦博士获得建院以来首个超过百万元经费的横向项目

2019.10.25 Dr. Xi Yang received an externally funded industrial project, the first industrial project more than 1M RMB in SAT

2019.12.18 博士生张冰峰等人的研究提高了自动驾驶汽车的安全性，并增强了其他依靠人工智能识别图像的技术

2019.12.18 Researchers including PhD student Bingfeng Zhang improved the safety of self-driving cars and enhanced other technologies that relied on the use of artificial intelligence to identify images

2023.2 SAT “探索与引领”系列学术报告启动第一期

2023.2 SAT "Exploring and Leading" academic seminar series launched the first session

2023.4.12 第一届西交利物浦大学—苏州大学机器人与高端医疗器械论坛

2023.4.12 The first workshop between XJTLU and Soochow University on Robotics and High—end Medical Instruments

2023.6 学院第一届本科毕业生中3/4进入全球Top100高校继续深造

2023.6 Three quarters of SAT first cohort UG graduates entered World Top 100 universities for further study

江苏省优秀毕业论文 Jiangsu Provincial Excellent FYP

2019年	施荣凯 Rongkai Shi	使用纺织制可穿戴手腕设备在车内进行交互的交互分类 Towards a Taxonomy of User-elicited In-vehicle Interactions Using Textile-based Wearable Wrist Interfaces
2022年	任沁心 Qinxin Ren	通过计算机图形学合成多摄像头视频数据集 Synthesis of Multi-Camera Video Datasets via Computer Graphics
	张成锐 Chengrui Zhang	应用机器学习评估草药面膜治疗痤疮的功效 Applying Machine Learning to Evaluate Herbal Masks in Acne Treatment Efficacy
2023年	周家宝 Jiabao Zhou	基于钙钛矿材料的人工智能突触薄膜晶体管的制备与应用研究 Research on the Preparation and Application of Artificial Intelligence Synapse Thin Film Transistor Based on Perovskite Materials
	龙俊坤 Junkun Long	对微缩世界在协作式虚拟现实中的探索 Exploration of WIM in Collaborative VR

2023.6 建院以来共有5名本科毕业生获得江苏省优秀毕业论文奖

2023.6 Five UG graduates awarded Jiangsu Provincial Excellent FYP since the founding of SAT

2020.1.1 肖继民教授获得建院以来首个超过五十万元经费的国家自然科学基金面上项目

2020.1.1 Prof. Jimin Xiao was awarded funding in a General Programme of the National Natural Science Foundation of China (NSFC), the first NSFC funded project more than 500K in SAT

2020.12.7 学院科研团队开发了一套能够直观反映车载储能设备节能数据的算法，成果发表于交通领域顶级期刊 *IEEE Transactions on Transportation Electrification*

2020.12.7 SAT researchers developed a set of algorithms which can intuitively reflect the energy—saving data of onboard energy storage devices (OESDs), and published in *IEEE Transactions on Transportation Electrification*, a top journal in the field of transportation

2020.12.31 人工智能产业研究院获评江苏省数据科学与认知计算工程研究中心创新平台

2020. 12.31 XJTLU AI University Research Centre awarded the innovation platform name of Jiangsu Province Engineering Research Centre of Data Science and Cognitive Computation at XJTLU

2022.11 学院四组队伍荣获第八届中国国际“互联网＋”大学生创新创业大赛铜奖

2022.11 Four teams from SAT won the bronze prize in the 8th China Internet+ College Students Innovation and Entrepreneurship Competition

第八届中国国际“互联网＋”大学生创新创业大赛
8th China Internet+ College Students Innovation and Entrepreneurship Competition

项目名称 Project	参与成员 Students
E-Nurse: 可穿戴医疗传感器与AI芯片 E-Nurse: Wearable Healthcare Sensors and AI chips	雷浩，王琦男，谢欣凯，曹一心，尹力，王海滨，李俊彦 Hao Lei, Qinan Wang, Xinkai Xie, Yixin Cao, Li Yin, Haibin Wang, Junyan Li
潮停元宇宙—数字停车智慧生态 ChaoTing—Parking Ecological Metaverse	吴明泽、赵睿翔 Mingze Wu, Ruixiang Zhao
ESGrow—3D城市农场智慧解决方案 ESGrow—3D Intelligent Solution: For Urban Farms	吕子涵，李煜，苏豪 Zihan Lyu, Yu Li, Hao Su
知水良测—机船协同的水环境智能化监测领航者 The Leader of Intelligent Water Monitoring with the Cooperation of Unmanned Aerial Vehicles (UAVs) and Unmanned Surface Vehicles (USVs)	王嘉成，曾钟情，杨正，郑沛洋，沙翔宇，吴赵东 Jiacheng Wang, Zhongqing Zeng, Zheng Yang, Peiyang Zheng, Xiangyu Sha, Zhaodong Wu

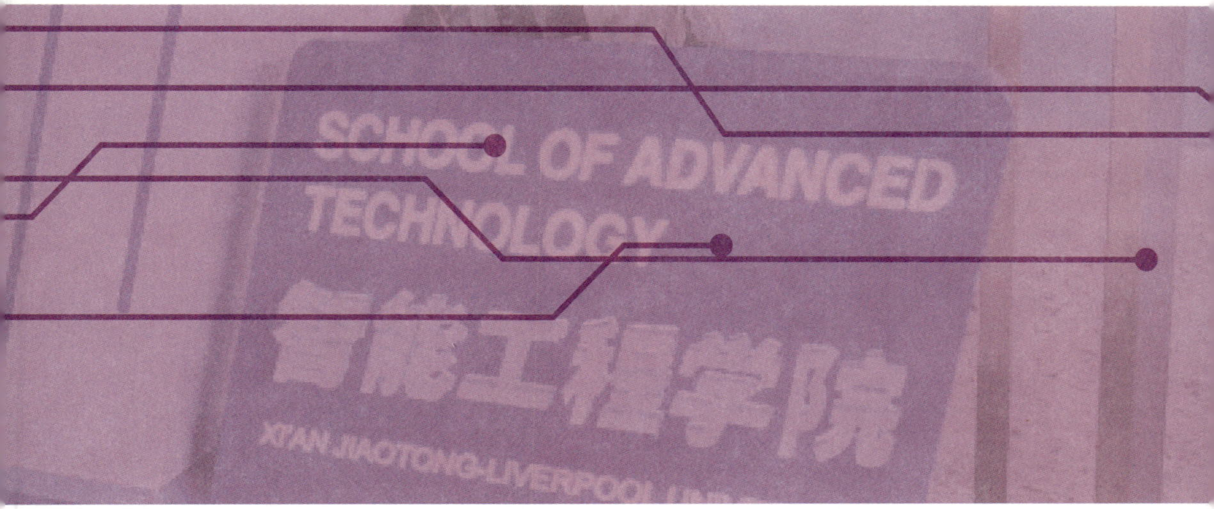

2022.12 王佳、林奇胜、方鲁睿、李圣辰、刘烨、李月、崔苗、王旭晨8人获江苏省人才项目，李圣辰获评江苏省“青蓝工程”优秀青年骨干、姑苏领军青年创新人才，张权获评苏州市优秀教育工作者，肖继民获评苏州工业园区优秀教育工作者，林奇胜获评独墅湖科教创新区国际型学科领军人才，余凌云、李圣辰、Thomas Selig、杨曦、王新珩、李月6人获评独墅湖科教创新区科教骨干人才，陈敏、刘雯、王佳、方鲁睿4人获评独墅湖科教创新区校企导师互聘访问工程师教师

2022.12 Jia Wang, Chee Shen Lim, Lurui Fang, Shengchen Li, Ye Liu, Yue Li, Miao Cui and Xuchen Wang awarded Jiangsu talent project; Shengchen Li awarded Jiangsu Qinglan talent and Gusu leading talent; Quan Zhang awarded Suzhou outstanding educator; Jimin Xiao awarded SIP outstanding educator; Chee Shen Lim, Lingyun Yu, Shengchen Li, Thomas Selig, Xi Yang, Xinheng Wang and Yue Li awarded SIP SEID key talent; Min Chen, Wen Liu, Jia Wang, Lurui Fang awarded SIP SEID visiting engineer teacher

2021.6.27 博士生李菁等人的研究成功用计算机识别出常见不规则文本，该论文在第27届国际神经信息处理大会上获最佳论文亚军，大会仅为四篇论文授奖

2021.6.27 Researchers including PhD student Jing Li proposed a new method to teach a computer to recognise irregular text common in everyday scenarios, and the paper was awarded the Best Paper Runner-Up at the 27th International Conference on Neural Information Processing, one of only four papers awarded at the conference

2021.9.3 赵春博士受邀出席第二十三届全国半导体物理学术会议作分会报告，是西交利物浦大学首次有教师受邀于会上进行报告分享

2021.9.3 Dr. Chun Zhao was invited to attend the 23rd National Semiconductor Physics Academic Conference to deliver a session report. This was the first time XJTLU academic staff invited to do oral presentation at the conference

2021.10 智能虚拟工程国际联合研究中心纳入国家国际科技合作基地信息管理系统管理

2021.10 The Virtual Engineering Center is included in the National International Science and Technology Cooperation Base Information Management System

师生故事

STORIES BETWEEN TEACHERS AND STUDENTS

许铭

MING XU

万紫千红总是春

ALL COLORS ARE ALWAYS SPRING

作为一位在西浦任教了十多年的教师，每每回忆起教过的学生，他们如同绽放的鲜花，一直在我的脑海里。他们背后的故事也一直激励着我努力前行。

As a teacher having worked with XJTLU for more than ten years, when I recall my past students, they are like stars in the sky shining to me. The stories of their diligence in their studies and research have impressed me so much.

2022.1 文辉清教授团队获中国产学研合作创新与促进奖

2022.1 Prof. Huiqing Wen's team won the China Industry University Research Cooperation Innovation and Promotion Award

2022.2.16 两名2021届电气工程专业本科毕业生的研究成果收录于2021年无线通信领域的顶级国际学术会议IEEE APS/URSI会议论文集

2022.2.16 Two BEng Electrical Engineering graduates' research findings included in the proceedings of the 2021 IEEE APS/URSI, the top international academic conference in the field of wireless communication

2022.6.8 孙捷教授两篇文章入选ESI高被引论文

2022.6.8 Two research articles of Prof. Jie Sun were listed as ESI highly cited papers

2022.7.31 林永义教授同时位列两指标（WoS Docs及Time Cited）2022年西浦十大高产作者首位

2022.7.31 Prof. Eng Gee Lim listed as the first one in the Top 10 authors within the university (in either indicators of WoS Docs or Times Cited) in 2022

2022.10 智能虚拟工程实验室获批为苏州市重点实验室

2022.10 Intelligent Virtual Engineering Lab approved as a Suzhou municipal key Lab

2022.6 文辉清教授获江苏省科技项目：基础研究项目（自然科学基金）——碳达峰碳中和技术创新项目，该项目经费300万元，是学院成立以来经费最多的纵向项目

2022.6 Prof. Huiqing Wen awarded a Jiangsu Science and Technology Programme: Fundamental Research Plan (Natural Science Foundation)—Carbon Peak Carbon Neutrality Technology Innovation Programme with RMB 3M fund, the largest governmental project in SAT

2022.10.20 西浦—友达联合实验室成立，这是建院以来首个经费达500万元的校企联合实验室

2022.10.20 XJTLU—AUO Collaborative Research Institute established, the first joint lab more than 5M in SAT

2023.5.15 博士生罗亦鸣、王佳林等人的研究成果获第18届国际虚拟现实连续体及其工业应用大会最佳论文奖

2023.5.15 Researchers including PhD students Yiming Luo and Jialin Wang won the Best Paper Award at the 18th International Conference on Virtual Reality Continuum and its Applications in Industry

2023.7.10 岳勇教授获西浦杰出博士生导师奖

2023.7.10 Prof. Yong Yue was awarded the outstanding supervisory support and research leadership award at XJTLU

2023.9.6 赵春博士获300万元经费项目，是学院成立以来经费最多的横向项目

2023.9.6 Dr. Chun Zhao received a RMB 3M external industrial funded project, the largest industrial project in SAT

2023.11.23 西浦—益航机器人校企联合研究中心成立

2023.11.23 Establishment of XJTLU—uGo Robotics Research Center

2023.11.23 文辉清教授入选斯坦福/爱思唯尔全球被引次数前 2% 研究学者名单

2023.11.23 Prof. Huiqing Wen named in Stanford/Elsevier's list of the top 2% of researchers cited worldwide

2024.1.1 学院6位老师获国家自然科学基金，其中重点项目1项，面上项目2项，青年科学家项目3项，立项数创学院历史成绩

2024.1.1 6 academic staff awarded National Natural Science Foundation of China (NSFC), with 1 key programme, 2 general programmes and 3 young scientist programmes, hitting new record in SAT

2024.1.1 西浦智能工程学院—红与蓝微电子校企联合研究中心成立

2024.1.1 Establishment of XJTLU—Red and Blue Microelectronics Collaborative Research Center

2024.4.1西浦—派光智慧感知人工智能联合研究中心成立

2024.4.1 Establishment of XJTLU—PAI Joint AI Research Center

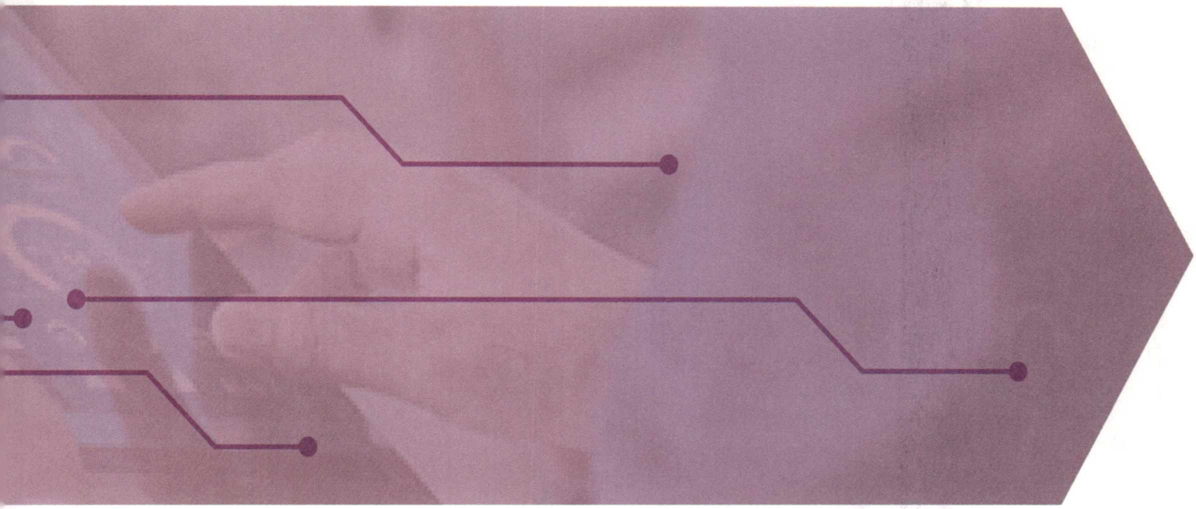

2024.6.30 过去五年学院外部经费总计高达6878万元，其中横向经费4173万元，纵向经费2705万元

2024.6.30 Total external funding up to RMB 68.78M in the past five years, including 41.73M industrial fund and 27.05M governmental fund

2024.7.2 学院5名教师获西浦学术卓越奖：林永义教授（学术成就卓越奖），Thomas Selig博士（教学卓越奖），杨瑞博士（科研卓越奖），杨曦博士（青年学者科研奖），赵春博士（科研指导奖）

2024.7.2 Five academic staff awarded XJTLU Academic Excellence Award: Prof. Eng Gee Lim (All-Round Academic Excellence Award), Dr. Thomas Selig (Teaching Excellence Award), Dr. Rui Yang (Research Excellence Award), Dr. Xi Yang (Early-Career Researcher Award) and Dr. Chun Zhao (Research Supervision Award)

我记得2020年10月，课题组的一篇论文被人工智能领域的著名国际期刊 *Pattern Recognition* 收录了。大家欢庆的同时，我却心系两位已经毕业的本科生沈默和郗晋同学。在此之前，他们与一位博士生进行多摄像机目标检测的研究，作为毕业设计的一部分。然而，在毕业设计刚开始不到三个月时，这位博士生却突然患病，不得不遵照医嘱休学半年。当时我们正在尝试一个大胆创新的想法，刚出现了非常好的效果。我深思熟虑后，将目光投在了两位学生身上。他们本来就是各自专业中的佼佼者，在全面接手了博士生的工作后，他们每天课后就来到实验室进行研究，甚至经常在晚上也守候在实验室里。在应对繁重的大四课程的同时，他们最终实现了计划中的各种算法，圆满地完成了科研任务。七月，当他们回到学校参加毕业典礼时，郗晋同学已在我的大力推荐下被宾夕法尼亚大学和密歇根大学安娜堡分校录取，沈默同学也被墨尔本大学录取。此时，博士生也恢复了健康，并重新承担起该项研究任务。当我们在我的办公室一起拍照留念时，我对两位学生充满了感激之情。我当时心里默默地想，只有继续努力工作，让这项工作成果早日发表，才能报答他们的帮助。

In October 2020, an article of my research team was accepted by the famous AI journal *Pattern Recognition*. When my PhD students celebrated the acceptance, I was missing two of my former FYP students Mo Shen and Jin Xi. They had worked with me to support my PhD student's research in multi-camera object detection. However, in the third month of their FYPs, my PhD student became very sick suddenly and had to suspend his study for six months. At that time, we were trying a novel idea and had some very promising initial results. After thinking about this heavy blow over night, I decided to hand over this work to these two FYP students. Since then, Mo Shen and Jin Xi came to our lab to work after their classes every day and spent their time there in the evening. Finally, they had implemented all the planned algorithms for this project, at the same time of achieving excellent academic performance in their Year-4 study. In July of the following year, when they attended the graduation ceremony, Jin Xi was accepted as an M.S. student at the University of Pennsylvania and University of Michigan, Ann Arbor, and Mo Shen was accepted by the University of Melbourne. At that time, my PhD student had recovered from his sickness and took back his research work from these two students. When we took photos together in my office, I felt gratitude to both students. I was thinking that the only way to express our thanks is to work hard to publish this work as early as possible.

在智能工程学院成立后的2020年，新冠疫情开始在世界范围内肆虐。2020年9月，国内疫情刚呈现可控趋势，学校便开始线下授课。我在讲授EEE339“数字系统设计与HDL”这门大四课程时，突然发现前排坐着一位“2+2”的学生滕德群。他在大二时就是我课堂上思维最活跃和最爱提问的学生。他告诉我，由于英国疫情严重，利物浦大学全部改为线上授课，他和大多数中国学生都回到了国内。他不满足在山东家里学习，而是在文星广场租了房子学习，白天到西交利物浦大学听课，晚上则参加利物浦大学的网课。从那时起，他成了我课堂上听课最专注的学生。由于利物浦大学是线上授课，在进行实验时，无法提供实验设备，只能使用仿真软件。考虑到“2+2”学生仍然是我们自己的学生，我为他提供了便利。在进行利物浦大学的设计作业和实验时，有不明白的地方，他也会请教我。利物浦大学教授他这门课的老师，正是与我有着十多年科研合作经历的史密斯教授（西浦第一位学术副校长）。我们的良好互动一直持续到学期结束。

In 2020, soon after the establishment of the School of Advanced Technology, the COVID-19 epidemic spread over the world. In September 2020, when the epidemic was just curbed in China, onsite classes resumed in XJTLU. When I taught a Year-4 module EEE339 “Digital System Design with HDL” one day, I found my “2+2” student Mr. Dequn Teng sitting in the front row of the lecture theatre. He was one of the most excellent students from two years previous. He told me that he, along with most Chinese students had come back to China due to the serious epidemic situation in Liverpool. He rented a flat in Wenxing Plaza, attended onsite classes at XJTLU in daytime and attended online UoL classes in the evening. Since then, he became the most serious student in my class again. We frequently discussed his UoL coursework and his instructor of the same module was my long-term research collaborator Prof. Jeremy Smith (the first VPAA of XJTLU). I also provided the equipment for him to do the lab, unlike other UoL students using simulation only. This happy experience with Dequn lasted until one day at the end of this module.

有一天上课时，滕德群同学来向我告别，说英国疫情形势好转，他要返回利物浦大学了。我们依依惜别，互道珍重。半年后，我知道了他被剑桥大学录取为硕士研究生的喜讯。2021 年 7 月底，当他返校参加毕业典礼时，特地来办公室看我并合影留念。2023 年 9 月的一天，我在上课时刚给 EEE339 的新同学们讲述了滕德群的故事，希望他们向学长学习。回到办公室后有人敲门。我一看竟然是滕德群。原来他借着回国开会的机会，又回到西浦来看我，此时他已是剑桥大学全额奖学金资助的博士研究生，举手投足之间已经展现出了一种年轻学者的风范。我们共进晚餐后已是晚上八点。他坚持要去当年上课的教室和图书馆拍照留念。他说在西浦的日子里过得充实、愉快。

On that day, he came to say farewell to me. He told me that the epidemic situation in the UK was better and he would go back to Liverpool. After half a year, I knew the good news that he was accepted as an MSc student at the University of Cambridge. In July 2021, when Dequn attended the graduation ceremony, he visited my office and took photos with me. One day in September 2023, after I told Dequn' s story to the new cohort EEE339 students in my class and returned to my office, someone was knocking at my door. It was Dequn who came to see me again. He was a fully funded PhD student in University of Cambridge at that time and came back to attend a conference in China. After the happy dinner with me, he said that he would go to the lecture theatres and library where he used to study and his dream came true.

作为老师，我认真地对待每一名学生的学习和毕业设计，并在学校和用人单位面前竭力推荐他们。2011 年 9 月，我的学生王桂芬从利物浦“4+1”硕士毕业，她请我写封推荐信，因为她要去深圳华为公司面试。后来，她告诉我，面试时她递交了一位利物浦大学老师的和我的推荐信。面试官当场打开并阅读了我亲手密封好的中文推荐信后说：“我们决定录用你。”

My students have impressed me so much in their motivation for learning and research. As a response, I am always keen to recommend my good students to universities and employers. One day my past FYP student Ms. Guifen Wang asked me to provide a reference letter for her job interview in Huawei. She just graduated from Liverpool with a M.Sc degree at that time. According to what Guifen recalled later, the Huawei interviewer opened and read my reference letter in front of her and told her that she was offered a position in Huawei.

当时，我在推荐信中写道：“由于她所尝试的方法我以前也没用过，所以她在相当程度上要独立地去学习和编程实现。最后王桂芬完成了杰出的工作……基于她的部分研究成果而写成的论文，在 ICIP 国际会议上发表。在王桂芬离开我校后，我学习和运行了她写的程序，发现她的代码风格简洁、条理清晰，运行起来很稳定。所以直到现在，我总是让我的研究生从读王桂芬写的毕业论文和程序代码起步。”2023 年底，我的学生潘枭楠请我给他写推荐信。他在研究中基于 Unity3D 的工具包，搭建了一个适用于虚拟场景中的多摄像机标定以及行人数据标注的平台，被广泛地应用于课题组的研究中。尽管他的学习成绩只有中上等，但我一直鼓励他申请一下名校。2024 年 4 月的一天，潘枭楠兴奋地告诉我，他同时被宾夕法尼亚大学和杜克大学计算机系录取。他一直说像在做梦，我说：“老师没在做梦。”我很高兴这几年我的学生有去宾大、哥伦比亚、CMU 和清华的，于是在我办公室的书柜前又增添了一张新的合影。

In my reference letter, I wrote: "Since she was required to try something which I had not used before, she had to learn and implement that method independently. Finally, she had done a good job......Part of her research work was published at an IEEE International Conference on Image Processing. After her leaving for M.Sc study, I have read and run her C/C++ codes. I found the codes were written in a compact and logical way and are very reliable in running. Due to this reason, I always ask my postgraduate students to start from reading Guifen's thesis and codes in their research." At the end of 2023, my FYP student Xiaonan Pan asked me to provide reference for him. His research is to synthesise multi-camera video datasets for pedestrian detection and tracking. Although he is not a top student in academic performance, I have identified his great potential for research and development. I encourage him to apply for some prestigious universities. One day in April 2024, Xiaonan came to my office excitedly. He told me that he was accepted by both the University of Pennsylvania and Duke University. He said that he felt like he was like dreaming. Then we took a new photo in front of my book shelf. To be able to help and witness my students' dreams coming true, I feel very happy.

师生故事

STORIES BETWEEN TEACHERS AND STUDENTS

肖继民
JIMIN XIAO

潜心科研路，矢志追梦人

DEDICATED TO CUTTING-EDGE AI RESEARCH, DETERMINED TO BE A DREAM-CHASER

五年光阴如白驹过隙，SAT不仅孕育了无数学子的梦想，见证了他们的成长，更为像我这样致力于科研的教师提供了坚实的臂膀和丰饶的土壤。作为 SAT的一名教授，我在学院的支持下，得以稳扎稳打地推进科研事业。

In the short span of five years, the School of Advanced Technology (SAT) has not only nurtured the dreams and growth of numerous students but also offered substantial support and resources and fertile ground to faculty members like myself who are dedicated to research. As a professor at SAT, I have been able to steadily advance my research career thanks to the support from the school.

2024 年，我的课题组在计算机视觉领域取得了显著的成果，在顶级会议 Computer Vision and Pattern Recognition Conference（CVPR）上发表了 4 篇论文，发表的文章涵盖了弱监督学习、半监督学习和增量学习等前沿方向，其中一篇更被评为 Highlight。这些研究涉及如何通过分离对象性和类别识别，实现持续学习的高效性；利用基于原型的物体像素挖掘技术；以及借助语言视觉模型作为骨干网络，显著提高弱监督语义分割的精度。我们还探索了密度递减特征扰动方法，为半监督语义分割开辟了新方向。这些研究不仅在理论上具有创新性，也在实际应用中展现了巨大的潜力。

In 2024, my research group made significant breakthroughs in the field of computer vision, publishing four papers at the Computer Vision and Pattern Recognition Conference (CVPR). These papers covered cutting-edge areas such as weakly supervised learning, semi-supervised learning, and incremental learning, with one paper being selected as a Highlight. Our research involved innovative methods for efficient continual learning through disentangled objectness learning and class recognition; mining prototype-based secondary discriminative pixels and leveraging vision-language models as a backbone network to significantly enhance weakly supervised semantic segmentation accuracy; and exploring density-descending feature perturbation techniques to pioneer new directions in semi-supervised semantic segmentation. These studies not only showcased theoretical innovations but also demonstrated strong potential for practical applications.

ICCV23
PARIS
CVF
IEEE
COMPUTER
SOCIETY

近年来，我们课题组在计算机视觉领域取得了显著进展，在国际期刊和会议上发表了大量高质量的论文，涵盖了TPAMI、IJCV、TIP、TMM、TCSVT、CVPR、ICCV、ECCV、AAAI、IJCAI等。这些成果不仅丰富了我们的研究内容，验证了课题组的科研能力，也大大提升了我们的学术影响力。

回顾课题组的成长历程，离不开初期的启动资金和资源支持，以及 SAT 对人工智能研究的远见卓识。课题组成立之初，我手握着来自学校人工智能研究中心的“人脸识别项目”启动资金，这为我提供了必要的研究支撑，使我能够迅速开展初期研究，并吸引了一批优秀的博士生加入团队，奠定了课题组稳步发展的基础。

Furthermore, in recent years, our research group has published numerous high-quality papers in various directions of computer vision in international journals and conferences , including TPAMI, IJCV, TIP, TMM, TCSVT, CVPR, ICCV, ECCV, AAAI, IJCAI, etc. These achievements have enriched our research content, validated the outstanding capabilities of my research team, and expanded our academic influence.

Looking back on the development of our research group, it is inseparable from the initial startup funding and resource support, as well as the foresight and insight, from SAT. At the beginning of the research group, I obtained the startup funding for the "Facial Recognition Project" from the University Artificial Intelligence Research Center, which provided essential research resources. This enabled me to quickly initiate preliminary research, attracting a group of outstanding doctoral students to join the team, laying a solid foundation for the steady development of the research group.

在学院的支持下，我带领课题组参加了 2019 年的 International Conference on Computer Vision（ICCV）。这次经历成为我们科研之路上的一个重要转折点。

2019 年秋天，我们怀揣着满腔热情踏上了前往 ICCV 会议的旅程。ICCV 是计算机视觉领域的顶级盛会，汇聚了全球最优秀的研究者和最新的科研成果。在会议期间，我们有幸聆听了许多重量级学者的报告，见识到了最前沿的研究成果。每一场报告都让我们感受到知识的震撼和灵感的迸发。我们与来自世界各地的研究者们热烈交流，讨论研究中的难题，分享各自的见解和经验。这些交流不仅拓宽了我们的视野，也让我们对自己的研究有了更深的理解和新的思路。通过这次会议，我们深刻体会到学术的真正意义——不仅是发表论文，更是通过交流和合作推动整个领域的进步。

With the support of the school, I led my research group to participate in the 2019 International Conference on Computer Vision (ICCV). This experience became a significant turning point in our research journey.

That autumn, we set off on our journey to the conference with a mixture of enthusiasm and nervousness. ICCV is a top-tier conference in the field of computer vision, gathering the world's best researchers and the latest scientific achievements. During the conference, we attended numerous presentations by prominent scholars and witnessed cutting-edge research. Each presentation left us in awe and sparked new ideas and inspiration. We engaged with researchers from around the globe, discussing challenges in our research, and sharing insights and experiences. These interactions not only broadened our horizons but also deepened our understanding of our own research and provided new perspectives. This conference made us realize the true essence of academia—not just publishing papers, but advancing the entire field through communication and collaboration.

回到学校后，我们将从ICCV 2019上获得的启发和经验融入自己的研究中。课题组仿佛注入了新的活力，工作质效迅速提升，接连产出了一些高质量的研究成果。我们的论文在顶级期刊和会议上频频亮相，课题组的影响力也逐步提升。从此，课题组真正步入正轨。每个成员都在各自的研究领域不断深耕，探索未知。我们明白，科研之路充满挑战，但正是这些挑战和不断学习让我们不断进步。

如今，回想起ICCV 2019，我不仅感激学院的支持，更为那段难忘的经历而自豪。它不仅是我科研生涯的一个重要里程碑，更是课题组共同成长的见证。在未来的科研道路上，我们会继续携手前行，不断追求卓越。

After returning to the university, we integrated the insights and experiences gained from ICCV 2019 into our own research. The quality of our group's work quickly improved, leading to the production of several high-quality research results. Our papers frequently appeared in top-tier journals and conferences, gradually increasing the influence of our research group. From that point on, our group truly found its stride. Each member continued to delve deeply into their respective research areas, exploring the unknown. We understood that the path of scientific research is full of challenges, but it is these challenges and the continuous learning that drive us to progress.

Looking back on ICCV 2019 now, I am not only grateful for the support from SAT but also proud of that unforgettable experience. It was not just an important milestone in my research career but also a testament to the collective growth of our research group. On our future research journey, we will continue to move forward together, relentlessly pursuing excellence.

AOC
2024
2024

随着科研成果的稳步产出，我有幸获得了来自政府和工业界超过千万元的研究资金支持。这些资金包括自然科学基金的面上项目、国家自然科学基金重点项目课题、国家重点研发计划课题、苏州市前沿技术研究项目的资金等。有了这些资金的支持，课题组得以购置先进的科研设备，吸引更多优秀人才加入我的团队。

As my research group continued to produce research outputs, I secured over ten million yuan in research funding from the government and industry, including projects supported by the National Science Foundation of China General Programme, National Science Foundation of China Major Programme, the National Key R&D Program of China, and Suzhou Science and Technology Development Planning Programme. These funds enabled us to acquire advanced research equipment and attract more talented individuals to join our team.

在课题组的建设过程中，SAT 提供的硬件资源，尤其是 GPU 的使用，使得我们的研究和实验进度得以大大提升。现代科研尤其是计算机视觉领域，对计算资源的要求非常高。SAT 提供的高性能计算资源让我们在短时间内完成了大量的实验和数据处理工作。

During the construction of my research group, the hardware resources provided by SAT, especially the use of GPUs, have greatly accelerated our research and experimentation processes. Modern research, particularly in the field of computer vision, demands extensive computational resources. With the high-performance computing resources of SAT, we can complete a large volume of experiments and data processing tasks in a short time.

除了硬件支持，SAT 还为我们搭建了一个学术交流的桥梁。学院定期组织的学术分享会议，为我们提供了思想碰撞的平台，我们与来自不同领域的专家学者交流讨论，分享最新的研究成果和技术进展。

Beyond hardware support, SAT also offers ample opportunities for academic exchanges. The academic sharing meetings organized regularly by the academy provide a broad platform for us to interact with experts and scholars from different fields, discuss our latest research findings, and exchange technological advancements.

在 SAT 成立的这五年里，我的努力和成果得到了学院、学校以及业内的广泛认可和高度评价。我获得了 SAT 的首届科研成就奖，入选苏州市高等院校、科研院所紧缺高层次人才计划，获评江苏省“333 工程”人才等荣誉称号。这不仅是对我个人科研成果的肯定，更是对整个科研团队辛勤耕耘的认可。与此同时，已经毕业的优秀学子们也在各自的领域茁壮成长，取得了令人瞩目的成就，他们的成功是对我们教育和科研体系的最好证明。其中，有的在中国石油大学（华东）和苏州大学任职副教授，有的在西交利物浦大学担任助理教授，还有的在香港理工大学和西北工业大学进行博士后研究，等等。他们在学术界继续发光发热，推动各自研究领域的发展。这些优秀学子的成功，也是 SAT 和课题组共同培养的结果。他们如同璀璨的星辰，激励着我们为培养更多杰出人才，为推动科研进步，不懈努力，继续前行。

Over the past five years, my efforts and achievements have also been widely recognized by the academy, the university, and the broader academic community. For instance, I received the 1st Research Achievement Award from SAT, as well as honors such as the High-Level Talent Plan for Universities and Research Institutes in Suzhou and the Jiangsu Province 333 Talent Project. These honors not only affirm my personal research accomplishments but also acknowledge the contributions of the entire research team. Meanwhile, our outstanding graduates have also achieved remarkable success in their respective fields, serving as a testament to our educational and research system. Some have become associate professors at China University of Petroleum (East China) and Soochow University, another has taken on the role of assistant professor at Xi'an Jiaotong-Liverpool University, and still others are conducting postdoctoral research at Hong Kong Polytechnic University, and Northwestern Polytechnical University. They continue to shine in the academic world, driving advancements in their research areas. The success of these distinguished alumni is a joint achievement of SAT and the research group. They are like brilliant stars, inspiring us to keep moving forward, tirelessly striving to cultivate more outstanding talents and advance scientific research.

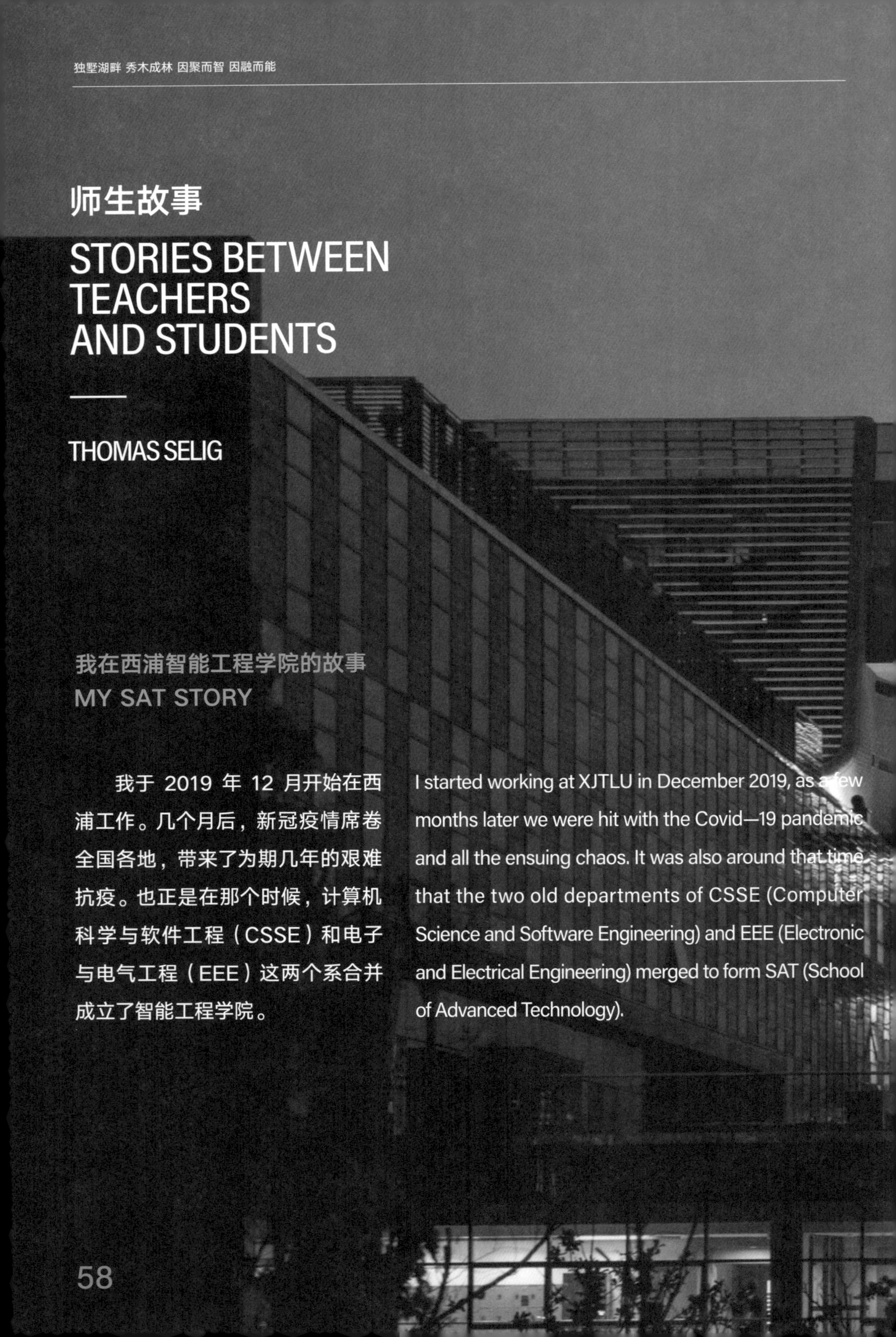

师生故事

STORIES BETWEEN TEACHERS AND STUDENTS

THOMAS SELIG

我在西浦智能工程学院的故事
MY SAT STORY

我于 2019 年 12 月开始在西浦工作。几个月后，新冠疫情席卷全国各地，带来了为期几年的艰难抗疫。也正是在那个时候，计算机科学与软件工程（CSSE）和电子与电气工程（EEE）这两个系合并成立了智能工程学院。

I started working at XJTLU in December 2019, as a few months later we were hit with the Covid—19 pandemic and all the ensuing chaos. It was also around that time that the two old departments of CSSE (Computer Science and Software Engineering) and EEE (Electronic and Electrical Engineering) merged to form SAT (School of Advanced Technology).

我加入西浦智能工程学院是出于个人和职业发展的双重原因。就我个人而言,我的妻子是无锡人,她的老家就在苏州旁边;我们的儿子当时只有一岁,所以想搬到离家更近的地方,有家人帮忙照顾。我岳父当时又正生病(谢天谢地,现在已经解决了),所以我们想住在附近,家人间相互照应。从工作角度来看,我当时在冰岛从事博士后研究,这是我自 2014 年 12 月获得博士学位以来的第二次博士后工作。我们非常希望有机会安定下来,担任更长期的角色。我妻子已经跟随我漂泊几年,一路从西班牙到法国、英国、冰岛,我觉得是时候跟着她回到她的祖国了。就我自己而言,我之前在中国旅行时去过苏州,我相信我会喜欢这里,事实证明我是对的。

I joined XJTLU and SAT for a mix of personal and professional reasons. From a personal perspective, my wife is from Wuxi, which is just next to Suzhou. We had a very young boy (one year old at the time), and wanted to move closer to some of our family for additional support. My father-in-law was also experiencing some health difficulties (thankfully now resolved), and so us living nearby would allow us to help as needed. From a professional perspective, I was engaged in a research postdoctoral position in Iceland at the time, my second such postdoc since completing my PhD degree in December 2014. The opportunity to settle down into a more permanent role was therefore most welcome. My wife having followed me around for a few years already, from Spain to France to the UK to Iceland, it felt only right that I should in turn follow her back to her home country. For myself, I had visited Suzhou on previous travels to China, and was confident I would enjoy living here, as it has proved.

西浦，尤其是智能工程学院，给我提供了非常愉快的工作环境。我也特别感谢这里给新员工提供的工作机会。我刚来第一年，被任命为计算机科学与软件工程专业的线上学习协调员。在新冠疫情期间，我们所有的教学任务都转到线上，需要全校老师积极应对、及时调整，大家都非常努力，我作为协调员也做了大量的工作。我真的很喜欢这个角色，尤其是学习不同的教育理论，以及如何最好地将其应用于在线学习。我认为，作为一所大学，我们很好地应对了挑战，想方设法保障了学生高质量的学习体验。

XJTLU, and SAT in particular, has proved an extremely pleasant environment to work in. I particularly appreciate the responsibility that is given to new staff here. In my first year, I was made e-learning coordinator for the CSSE department. With the pandemic situation, this was certainly a busy period in that respect, as all our teaching immediately moved online, requiring a lot of effort from staff across the University to react and adjust to the change. I really enjoyed the role, in particular learning about the different educational theories and how they can best be applied to online learning. I think that as a University we responded well to the challenge, and managed to maintain a high quality of learning experience for our students.

西浦非常重视学生的学习。我们的执行校长席教授对教育充满热情（尤其是最近的人工智能发展——他有自己的数字孪生），这也渗透到了我们的教职员工身上。在我工作过的其他大学，大家有时认为教学不是最重要的，但西浦并非如此。对教学的重视在智能工程学院得到了回应。我们学院与教育发展部门的同事合作，每周组织关于学习和教学各方面的研讨会。我们还要求所有新员工取得高等教育教学和辅助学习研究生证书（PGCert）。我个人在两年前就通过课程、取得了证书，我觉得我真的从各种研讨会上学到了很多，这让我成为一名更好的老师。正如我们的院长林永义教授在最近的智能工程学院会议中所说的，“教学第一”。

In general, I think the emphasis the university places on our students' learning is great. Our executive president, Prof. Youmin Xi, is really passionate about education (in particular the recent AI developments—he has his own digital twin), and this filters down to our teaching staff. Other universities I have worked at have sometimes viewed teaching as a necessary inconvenience, but that is very much not the case here. This focus is echoed within SAT. Our School organises weekly workshops on various aspects of learning and teaching, in coordination with our colleagues from the Educational Development Unit. We also require all our new staff to pass the PGCert programme (Postgraduate Certificate in Teaching and Supporting Learning in Higher Education). I myself graduated from this programme about two years ago, and I feel I really learned a lot from the various workshops, which has made me a better teacher. As our Dean, Prof. Eng Gee Lim, stated at SAT's most recent away day, "Teaching comes first".

作为一名中文水平非常有限的外国老师，我在智能工程学院乃至西浦备受欢迎。这里大多数活动都是用英语进行的，即使是中文活动，也会提供英文字幕。当然，我们所有的员工都能说流利的英语（超过 90% 的 SAT 员工有国际经验），与他们沟通毫无障碍。如有需要，我们出色的行政人员也随时能为我提供帮助。我很幸运，我的妻子还有我的中国博士生也在需要时给我提供了额外的帮助。从教学的角度来看，我们学生的英语大多都很好，尤其是本科生。我教一门三年级的课程，学生们已经有了足够的西浦学习的经验，并且已经习惯了用英语学习。但我仍然发现自己在上课时经常不得不提醒自己说得慢一点！从研究的角度来看，这有时会很有挑战性，尤其是需要用中文撰写项目申请时。我特别自豪的是，在学院和大学的支持下，我在 2021 年成功获得了国家自然科学基金青年科学家基金。

As an international staff with very limited Chinese, I have always been made to feel very welcome by SAT and XJTLU. Efforts are made to run most events in English, and even for the Chinese events there are usually subtitles available which allow me to follow. And of course, all of our staff speak excellent English (more than 90% of SAT staff has international experience), so there are no issues communicating with them. Our wonderful Professional Service Staff are always on hand to help if necessary. My wife has also been brilliant when needed, and I am fortunate to have recruited a Chinese PhD student who provides added support. From a teaching perspective, our students' English is mostly very good, at least for the Undergraduate students I teach. It helps that I have a Year 3 module, meaning the students already have enough experience of XJTLU's learning environment, and are used to studying in English. Although I do still find myself often having to remind myself to speak more slowly during lectures! From a research perspective, it can sometimes be challenging, especially when it comes to writing grant applications in Chinese. As such, I am particularly proud that, with support from the School and University, I successfully obtained an NSFC Young Scientists fund in 2021.

我自 2020 年 9 月起，在智能工程学院的主要行政职务是计算机科学专业（研究型硕士）的专业主任。我的职责主要包括审查申请和面试潜在的候选人，我很喜欢。特别是，了解更多传统的中国大学非常有趣。我记得当我第一次看到其中一个计算机科学专业学生的成绩单时，我非常惊讶，上面列出了包括体育和马克思主义发展史等课程！这个职责一开始挑战性比较大，但我现在已经驾轻就熟。该专业近年来成绩喜人，在近两届学生中，超过一半的学生以优异等次毕业。近两年，我还主持或共同主持了智能工程学院的硕士开放日，向有意向的申请人介绍我们的学院和研究生课程。在学院的宣讲结束后，我们有机会亲自与这些申请者会面，进行一对一的咨询解答，我发现这对了解他们的关切和需求非常有帮助（尤其是在当前中国充满挑战的就业市场上）。

My main management role at the moment in SAT is serving as Programme Director of the Master of Research in Computer Science programme, a position I have held since September 2020. My responsibilities mostly involve reviewing applications and interviewing potential candidates, which I enjoy. In particular, it has been very interesting to learn about more traditional Chinese universities. I remember being very surprised the first time I saw a transcript from one of these, with listed courses including Physical Education and History of Marxism, in a Computer Science major! While this role was quite a steep learning curve in the beginning, I feel I have adapted well. The programme has achieved excellent results in recent years, with over 50% of our students in the last two cohorts graduating with a distinction. I have also hosted or co-hosted SAT's Master's Open Day the last two years, presenting our School and its Postgraduate programmes to prospective applicants. After the School presentation, we have had the opportunity to meet these applicants in person for one-on-one consultations, which I found highly valuable in terms of understanding their priorities and concerns (particularly around the currently challenging job market in China).

到目前为止，我在智能工程学院和西浦度过了非常愉快的时光，我也希望它能继续下去。

Overall, I would say that my time in SAT and XJTLU has been a highly pleasurable experience to date, and I hope it will continue going forward.

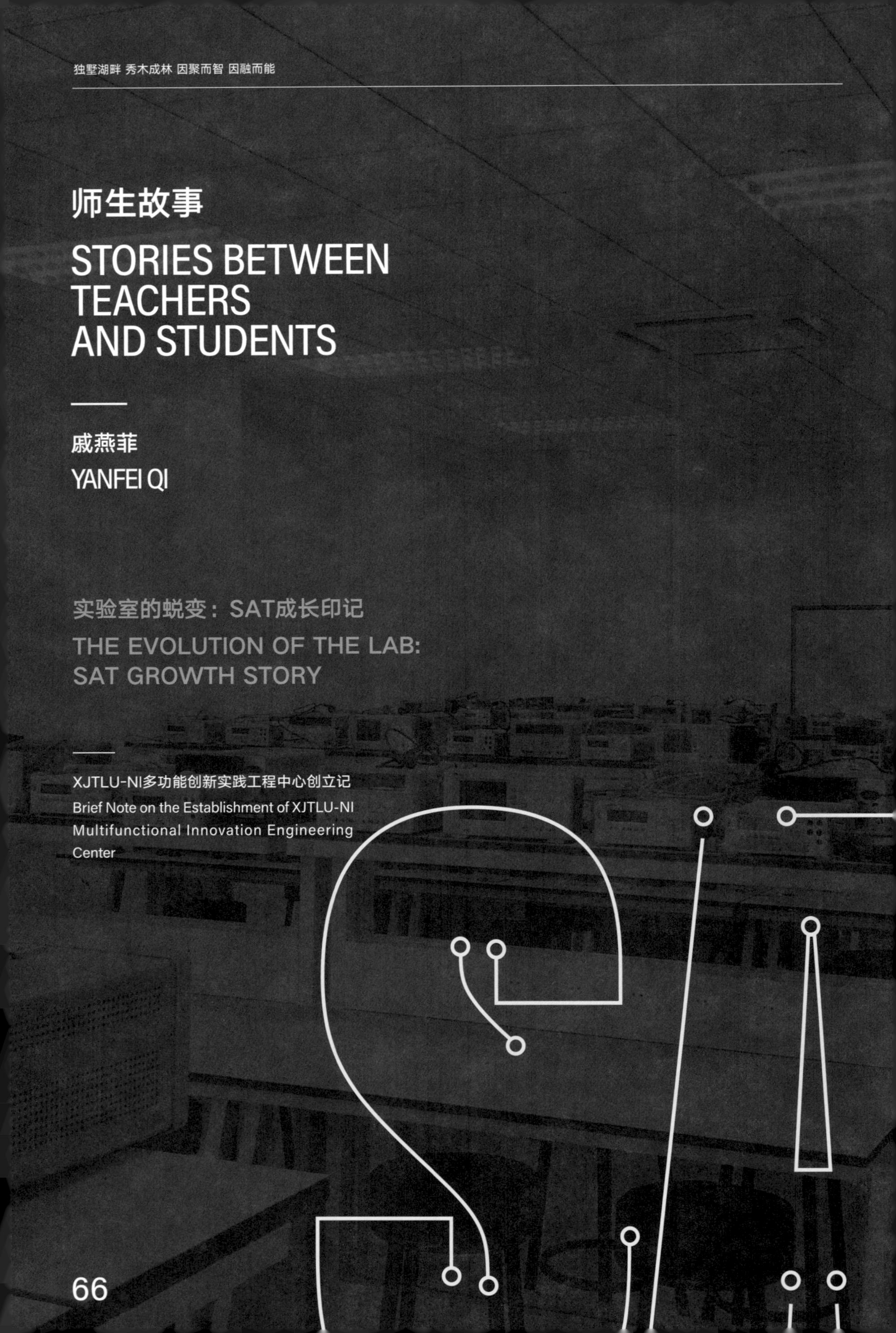

师生故事

STORIES BETWEEN TEACHERS AND STUDENTS

戚燕菲

YANFEI QI

实验室的蜕变：SAT成长印记

THE EVOLUTION OF THE LAB: SAT GROWTH STORY

XJTLU-NI多功能创新实践工程中心创立记

Brief Note on the Establishment of XJTLU-NI Multifunctional Innovation Engineering Center

在智能工程学院这座充满智慧与创新的殿堂里，有一个特别的地方，那就是我们熟知的教学实验室，它见证了学院从稚嫩到成熟的每一步。这个实验室不仅是学子们追逐梦想、探索知识的“圣地”，更是学院成长与变迁的忠实记录者。它的蜕变不仅仅是硬件设施的更新换代，也是学院在科研与教学领域持续投入和不懈努力的证明。更重要的是，这个实验室还代表着学院教育理念的深化与升华，象征着对学生实践能力、创新思维以及综合素质培养的高度重视。

In the sanctuary of wisdom and innovation, the School of Advanced Technology houses a special place—our well-known teaching laboratory. It has witnessed the school's growth from infancy to maturity. This laboratory is not only a"holy land"where students pursue their dreams and explore knowledge but also a faithful recorder of the school's development and transformation. Its evolution signifies not only the upgrading of hardware facilities but also the school's continuous investment and unwavering efforts in scientific research and teaching. More importantly, this laboratory represents the deepening and sublimation of the school's educational philosophy, symbolizing the high importance placed on students' practical abilities, innovative thinking, and comprehensive quality cultivation.

五年前，当智能工程学院刚刚成立时，坐落在 EE 二楼的 4 间单间电子实验室便是我们的起点。每间约百平米的实验室里，整齐地排列着 28 张工作台，每张工作台上都配备着直流电源、示波器、台式万用表等实验设备。那时的我们，就在这样的环境中，开始了电气学习之旅。每当回忆起那段时光，我总会想起老师们忙碌的身影，他们穿梭在每个实验室中，耐心细致地讲解着每一个知识点。然而，由于实验条件的限制，很多实验项目都无法开展。学院的领导层深知，一个先进的实验室不仅是培养学生实践能力的场所，更是促进科研创新和跨学科交流的重要平台。

Five years ago, when the School of Advanced Technology was just established, our starting point was four separate electronic laboratories located on the second floor of EE Building. Each laboratory, approximately 100 square meters, was neatly arranged with 28 benches, each equipped with devices such as a DC power supply, oscilloscope, and desktop multi-meters. It was in this environment that we embarked on our journey of electrical learning. Whenever I recall those days, I always remember the busy figures of our teachers, who patiently explained every piece of knowledge as they moved through each laboratory. However, due to limitations in experimental conditions, many projects could not be carried out. The School' s leadership was well aware that an advanced laboratory is not only a place to cultivate students' practical abilities but also an important platform for promoting scientific research innovation and interdisciplinary exchange.

随着学院的不断发展壮大，大二学生的数量从四百多人骤增到六百多人，这带来的资源分配压力让新型实验室的建设成为了一项迫切的需求。在获得校方的大力支持后，一场关于新型实验室建设的讨论在学院内部悄然展开。那是一个炎热的夏天，领导们带领我们一次次地跑到现场，构思规划实验室的设计方案。从布局到设备配置，从运行方式到管理模式，每一个细节都被老师们及实验员们认真讨论和反复推敲。经过无数次的讨论和碰撞，学院终于勾勒出了一幅开放式多功能实验室的蓝图。这个实验室不仅要具备传统实验室的功能，解决资源限制问题，还要能够容纳各种创新性的实验项目，具备学院特色。

As the school continued to grow and expand, the number of Year 2 students increased sharply from over 400 to more than 600, which brought significant pressure on resource allocation. The construction of a new type of laboratory became an urgent need. With strong support from the university, a discussion on constructing a new laboratory quietly unfolded within the school. It was a hot summer day. Under the leadership of the deans, we repeatedly visited the site to conceptualize and plan the design of the laboratory. From layout to equipment configuration, from operation mode to management mode, every detail was carefully discussed and repeatedly deliberated by teachers and technicians. After countless discussions and collisions, the School finally outlined a blueprint for an open and multifunctional laboratory . This laboratory was designed to not only fulfill the functions of a traditional laboratory and address resource constraints but also accommodate various innovative experimental projects with unique school characteristics.

方案确立后，实验室的建设开始启动。校园管理办公室 CMO 对实验室进行了科学合理的规划，并不厌其烦地与学院沟通需求并修改方案。从工作台的布局到家具的选购，每一个细节都经过反复考量，力求兼顾功能性、安全性及舒适性。最终，在一个阳光明媚的日子里，新型实验室正式竣工。这间占地约 500 平方米的实验室里，整齐地排列着 150 张工作台，能够同时容纳 300 名学生进行实验。同时，学院还配套采购了 150 套先进的实验设备和仪器，为师生们提供了优质的教学和科研环境。该集成多合一工业级仪器具备可编程 I/O 测量功能，可通过 FPGA 控制，并能实现远程控制。其配套含有几乎可覆盖电子信息与电气类专业核心课程的完整实验方案，并支持第三方实验板卡以满足跨学科实验教学。这一设备的引入一方面解决了学院教学实验室时间空间限制的问题，同时也为教学模式的创新提供了可能性，让学生在具备基本理论知识和实验技能的基础上，能够开展自主综合设计实验。

After the plan was finalized, the lab construction began. Campus Management Office (CMO) conducted scientific and reasonable planning for the laboratory, communicating with the school repeatedly to understand needs and modify the plan. From the layout of benches to the selection of furniture, every detail was carefully considered to ensure functionality, safety, and comfort. Finally, on another sunny day, the new laboratory was officially completed. This approximately 500-square-meter laboratory houses 150

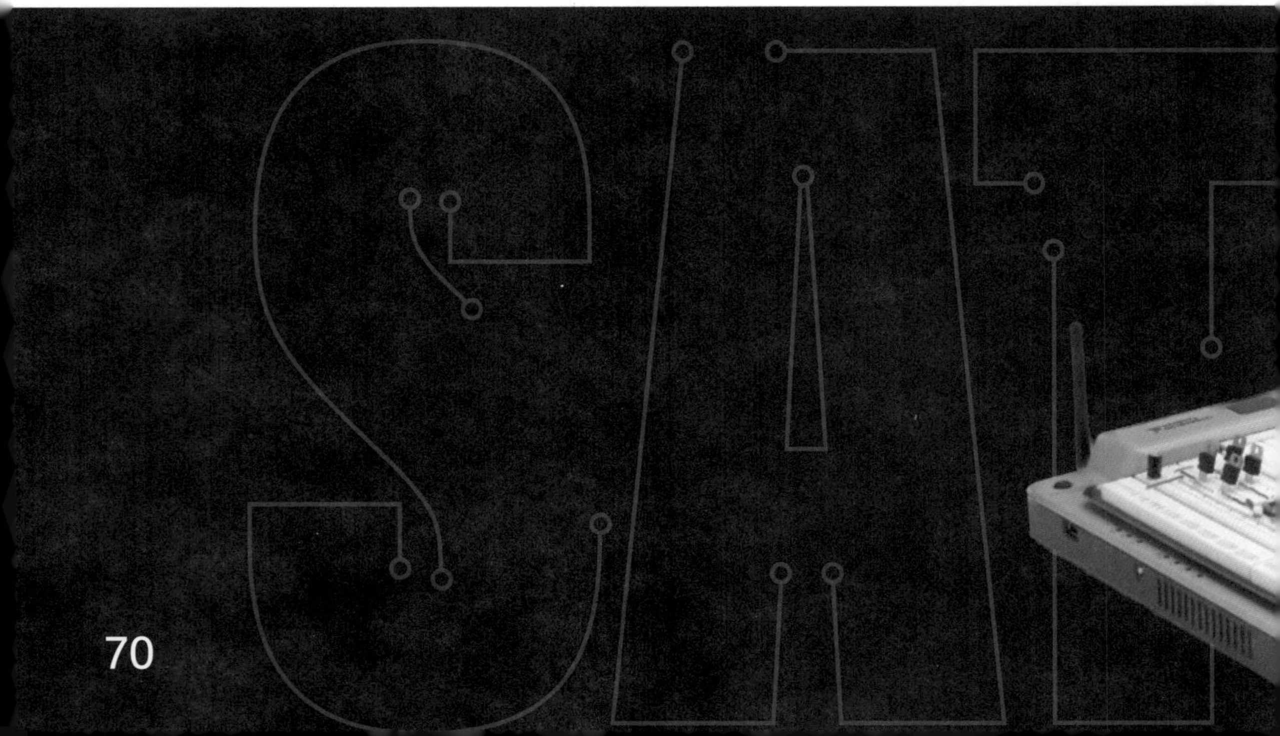

workstations that can accommodate 300 students for experiments simultaneously. In addition, the school also purchased 150 sets of advanced experimental equipment and instruments , providing a high-quality teaching and research environment for teachers and students. This integrated industrial-grade instrument features programmable I/O measurement capabilities, FPGA control, and remote control. It comes with a complete experimental program that covers the core courses of Electronic Information and Electrical Engineering while supporting third-party experimental boards to meet interdisciplinary experimental teaching needs . The introduction of this equipment not only solves the issues of time and space constraints in the school's teaching laboratories but also provides possibilities for innovative teaching models, allowing students to conduct independent comprehensive design experiments based on their basic theoretical knowledge and experimental skills.

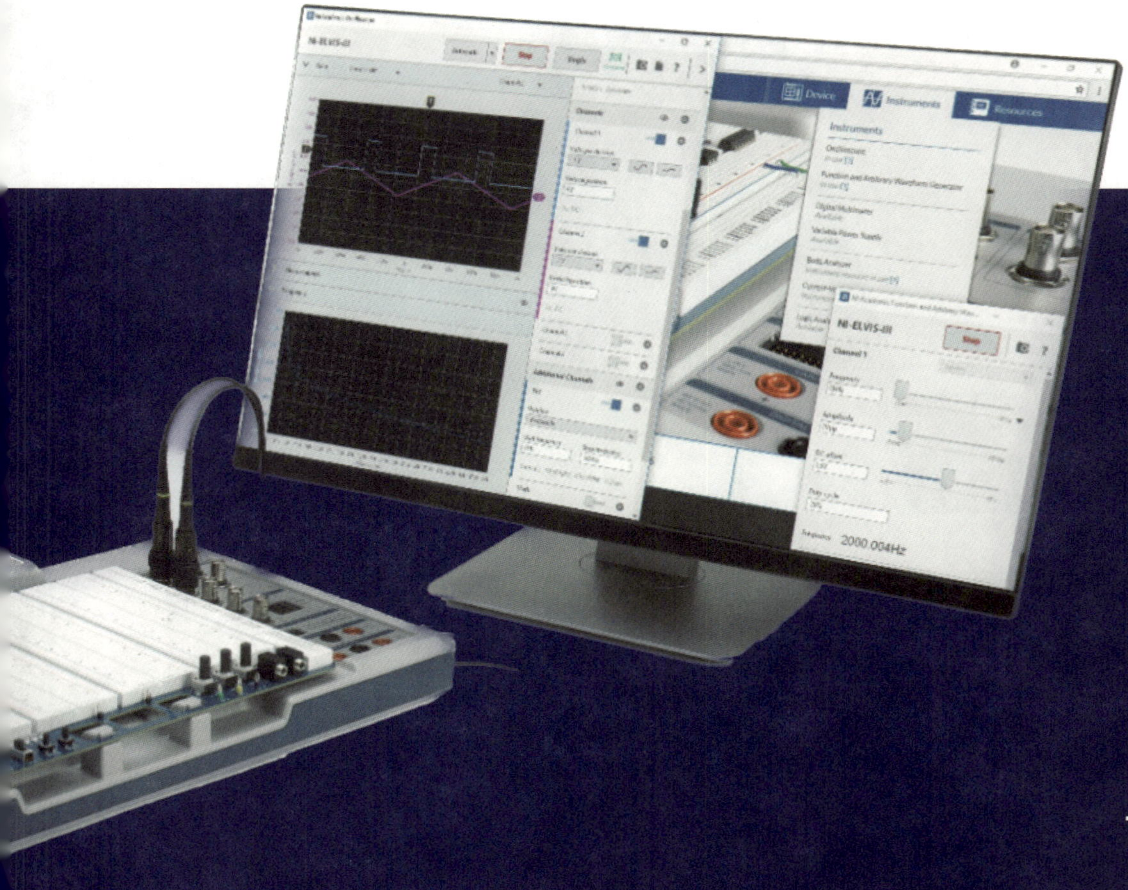

SAI LAB

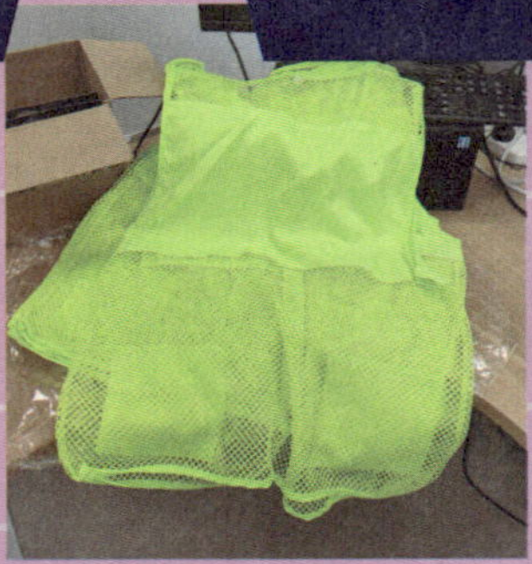

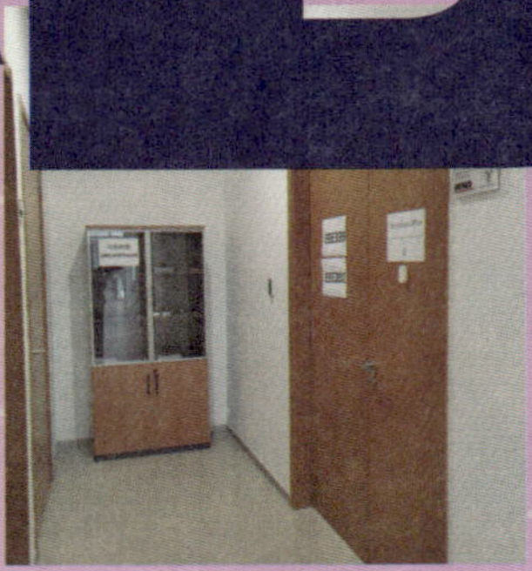

实验室建成后，它的变化不仅仅是学院硬件设施升级的象征，更是学院服务理念变革的缩影，展现了学院对于教学科研工作的重视和投入。学院鼓励师生们充分利用实验室资源，开展各种创新性的实验项目。在该共享服务理念的引导下，学院实验员团队迅速调整了分工，形成了由资深实验员孔繁华带领下的教学分队，全员参与支持学院教学工作并支持该开放式实验室的日常运行。除了支持爆场安排的学院各类实验，为实现开放式管理，实验员小伙伴们在实践中迸发了诸多管理创意，包括办公室内每日传递的“接待处”标牌、分类整齐鲜明的元器件盒子、各类实用贴心的实验小提示以及让 TA 和教师“无处遁形”的彩色小马甲等。每种小创意的背后都是工作人员对优化工作和提升服务的思考，这是对学院理念的真实践。

After the completion of the laboratory , its transformation is not only a symbol of the school's efforts to continually upgrade its hardware but also a microcosm of the transformation of the School's service philosophy, demonstrating the School's emphasis and investment in teaching and research. The school encourages teachers and students to make full use of the laboratory resources to carry out various innovative experimental projects. Guided by the shared service philosophy, the division of labor for the laboratory technician team was quickly adjusted. A teaching team led by the senior technician Fanhua Kong was formed, with all members participating in supporting the School's teaching work and the daily operation of the open laboratory. In addition to supporting various experiments arranged by the School, to achieve open management, the laboratory technicians have come up with many innovative management ideas in practice , including the "reception" sign passed daily in the office, neatly classified and distinctive component boxes, various practical and thoughtful experimental tips, as well as colorful vests that ensure TAs and teachers have "nowhere to hide." Behind each small idea, there is the staff's thinking on optimizing work and improving services, which is a true practice of the School's philosophy.

如今，这座多功能实验室已经成为学院的一张闪亮名片。越来越多的师生开始参与到实验室的项目中来，实验室年度访问量高达近两万次。师生在这里开展各种创新性的实验项目，探索着未知的领域。从四小间传统教学电子实验室到如今一大间现代化工程实践中心的转变，不仅体现了学院整体实力的提升，更推动着学院不断向前发展。

Nowadays, this multifunctional laboratory has become a shining business card of SAT. An increasing number of teachers and students have begun to participate in projects at this center. Annual visits are close to nearly 20,000. Here, they conduct various innovative experimental projects and explore unknown fields. The transformation from four small traditional teaching electronics laboratories to one large modern engineering center not only reflects the overall strength enhancement of the college but also drives its continuous development.

未来，随着科技的不断进步和学院的不断发展，这座多功能实验室将继续秉持共享服务的理念，为师生们提供更加优质、高效、便捷的教学和科研服务。它将继续见证着学院的成长与变迁，成为我们心中永恒的记忆和骄傲。

In the future, with the continuous progress of technology and the development of the School, this multifunctional center will continue to uphold the concept of shared services, providing teachers and students with more quality, efficient, and convenient teaching and research services. It will continue to witness growth and school changes, while providing an eternal memory and a sense of pride in our hearts.

师生故事

STORIES BETWEEN TEACHERS AND STUDENTS

尹力
LI YIN

情系西浦 山海相约

MEET IN THE FUTURE WITH SINCERE HEART

2023 年 3 月 6 日，我在西交利物浦大学（简称“西浦”）智能工程学院的博士生涯正式结束了。总觉得来日方长，却不知岁月清浅，时节如流。回首在西浦的四年时光，曾笑过，哭过，憧憬过，迷惘过。目光所及，皆是回忆，感恩生命中的每一次相遇。

On March 6, 2023, my doctoral journey in the School of Advanced Technology (SAT), at Xi'an Jiaotong-Liverpool University (XJTLU), was officially completed. Looking back on my four years at XJTLU, I have laughed, cried and dreamed. I am grateful for every encounter in my life.

天假其便 妙不可言
FATE IS WONDERFUL

与西浦的缘分可追溯到 2018 年，我在新南威尔士大学光伏与可再生能源专业学习期间，我的同门师兄正是毕业于西交利物浦大学。他流利的语言能力、缜密的逻辑思维、过硬的专业知识给我留下了很深的印象。于是，当我萌生了继续读博深造的想法时，我第一时间想到了西交利物浦大学。在通过了赵策洲教授及赵春教授的面试之后，两位导师给予了我很大的肯定与鼓励，于是在 2019 年 1 月 1 日，我顺利地开启了我的博士生涯。

My connection with XJTLU dates back to 2018 when I was studying Photovoltaics and Renewable Energy at the University of New South Wales. A senior classmate, who graduated from XJTLU, left a deep impression on me with his fluent language skills, meticulous logical thinking, and strong professional knowledge. Thus, when I entertained the idea of pursuing a doctoral degree, XJTLU was my immediate choice. After a successful interview with Professor Cezhou Zhao and Professor Chun Zhao, both supervisors affirmed and encouraged me greatly. On January 1, 2019, I embarked on my doctoral journey.

师者如光，微以致远
SUPERVISORS GUIDING ME TO DISTANT HORIZONS

我的导师一共有三位，分别是赵策洲教授、林永义教授以及赵春教授。三位导师在我的学术生涯及人生道路中都给予了我非常多的指导和帮助。

I was fortunate to have three supervisors: Professor Cezhou Zhao, Professor Eng Gee Lim and Professor Chun Zhao. Each provided significant guidance and support throughout my academic and personal journey.

在赵策洲教授身上，我看到了老一辈科研人的风骨。他不但在学术上传道授业解惑，同时也告诫我学术需要有求真务实的态度。遗憾的是，赵教授在 2021 年 4 月 15 日因病不幸离开了我们，而彼时我在学术上还没有任何成果产出，这让我感到深深的自责和懊悔。我想，时至今日，我的学术水平距离赵教授当初对我的期望也必是有所差距的。每思及此，我都深有忝列门墙之感，但路漫漫其修远兮，吾必铭记赵教授的教诲，上下求索。

I saw the spirit of the seasoned researcher in Professor Cezhou Zhao. He not only imparted academic wisdom but also emphasized the importance of a sincere and pragmatic approach. Regrettably, Professor Zhao passed away on April 15, 2021, before I had made any significant academic achievements, leaving me with deep regret and self-reflection. I feel deeply ashamed for not fullfilling Professor Zhao's initial expectation during his time, yet I am determined to retain his teachings in my mind and continue seeking knowledge.

林永义教授同时也是学院的院长，他在繁忙的教学及行政任务中，仍然会抽出不多的休息时间，定期与我们回顾近期的学术进展及讨论未来的研究方案。并且在我最迷茫的时候，是他给予我莫大的安慰和鼓励。记得博二下半学期开始的组会上，按照惯例，每位同学要汇报目前已发表及在投的成果。其他同学都有已被接收的成果，甚至有人还有两篇以上，而只有我，由于前期标准器件的摸索及表征耗费了太多时间，在当时连已投的成果都没有，在汇报中我羞愧难当。林教授安慰我说，他能够看到我为了更好的成果在前期所付出的努力，前期的积淀是后期成功的基础；学术过程虽需要一点点运气和机遇，但只要我坚持下去，不忘初心，终能够有所得。林教授的话，让我释怀了不少，也让我更有了向前的动力。终于，在林教授的鼓励和帮助下，我的成果发表在了行业顶刊《先进能源材料》上。

Professor Eng Gee Lim, then and now the Dean of the School, in spite of his busy schedule, still regularly took time to review our recent academic progress and discuss future research plans. During a period of confusion, his comfort and encouragement were invaluable. I vividly remember a group meeting in my second year when each student reported their published results. I had spent too much time on extensive experimentation and characterization efforts so had nothing to report on. Professor Lim reassured me, acknowledging my efforts to lay the groundwork for future success would bear fruit. His words provided solace and renewed my determination. Eventually, with Professor Lim's guidance, my research was published in the top journal *Advanced Energy Materials*.

在这四年的科研生涯中，我和赵春教授的交流是最多的。他给了我极大的耐心和信任，让我大胆地研究自己认为对的方向，在此过程中他又指导我小心严谨地求证。而且赵教授在生活中也给予我无微不至的关心，赵教授在我博一时的一次聚会上对我妻子说读博是一件很辛苦、困难的事情，需要家里充分理解和支持。因此在这四年中，我虽然收入微薄且对家庭照顾不周，我的妻子依然能够理解体谅我，直到我毕业时她才告诉我，其实一早赵教授就和她聊过这些。因为年轻气盛，我在科研瓶颈期也与赵教授有过争执甚至怄气，是他一直包容我，并告诉我年轻人有傲气有学术坚持是好事，只要是为了追求真理。"落其实者思其树，学其成时念吾师。"感谢赵春教授一直以来的鼓励、帮助、关心乃至鞭策，在离开学校进入社会后的很多场合，我都能想起他当初给予我的教导，这也一直指引着我成为更好的自己。

Throughout my research career, I had extensive interactions with Professor Chun Zhao, who demonstrated immense patience and trust. He encouraged me to boldly pursue directions I believed in, guiding me through meticulous verification processes. Outside academia, he offered unwavering care and support. At a gathering during my first year, he spoke to my wife about the challenges and sacrifices of pursuing a doctoral degree, emphasizing the need for understanding and support at home. Therefore, in the past four years,although my income was low and I didn't take good care of my family,my wife still understood me.It was only when I graduated that she told me that professor Zhao had talked about this with her early.Despite my youthful arrogance and occasional disagreements during research bottlenecks, he remained tolerant, recognizing the value of academic persistence and passion. His continuous encouragement and occasional reprimands have guided me in numerous professional and personal encounters since graduation.

愿岁并谢，与长友兮
MAY WE JOURNEY TOGETHER THROUGH THE YEARS, WITH ENDURING FRIENDSHIP

在这段美妙的旅程中，我也很幸运地结交了许多志同道合的同学和朋友，他们给了我很多的帮助和启迪。我们一起经历悲喜，一起走过荆棘，这些碎片共同拼接成我最美好的回忆。记得博一刚开始做器件辐射的实验，师兄带我去 EE 楼辐射实验室学习，我们俩穿着厚厚的铅衣，蹲下去探出头把器件固定在辐射源上端，两个人还不小心碰到了头，从实验室出来一人头上一个大包相视而笑；记得为了一个实验结果的对错，我们师兄弟姐妹几个人在 IR 会议室争论了三四个小时，错过了晚饭时间，最后只能回到宿舍一人吃一碗炒方便面；记得在遇到瓶颈时，几个兄弟一起去文萃吃烧烤喝啤酒，抒发心中的困惑与迷惘，喝醉后回家还错过了第二天免费的春游活动……毕业后每每想起这些，都哑然失笑，倍感亲切。人生海海，山山而川，我与同门必当于道各努力，千里自同风。

During this remarkable journey, I was fortunate to meet many like-minded classmates and friends who provided invaluable help and inspiration. Together, we shared joys and sorrows, traversed obstacles, these fragments piece together into my most valuable experiences and memories. I fondly recall incidents such as experimenting with radiation devices in the EE lab, heated debates over experimental results, and late-night gatherings for barbecue and beer, where we vented our frustrations and uncertainties. These reminiscences never fail to bring a smile to my face and a warm feeling of camaraderie. As we continued to strive toward our respective goals, I am reminded of the unity and determination we shared.

博学明道，笃行任事
LIGHT AND WINGS

除了导师和同学朋友的支持，我也感受到了学校及学院的关怀。在这里，我不单是一个科研工作者，学校还安排我担任助教的工作。助教工作不但能够让我巩固基础知识，而且在与同学们及任课老师的交流中，也提升了自己的授课能力。我经常会在微信中看到之前带过的同学申请到了很好的硕博学校，看着他们在异国提升自己，我也与有荣焉。同时，每一位同学在学习期间，学校还提供赴英国利物浦大学进行为期 3—6 个月免费研究访学的机会以及会议经费资助。在参会及访学期间，我们的学术交流圈大大拓宽，同时视野也逐步拓展。不仅如此，学校还给每一位同学提供生活及心理咨询导师，解决了每一位同学在科研中的后顾之忧。学院也会定期举行学术海报的评比，给予大家总结和锻炼的机会。正是在学校及学院提供的良好的氛围下，我们才能够更加全身心地投入到科研中，实验室的同学们也才能硕果累累。云山苍苍，江水泱泱，我院之风，山高水长。

In addition to the support of my supervisors, classmates and friends, I appreciate the care and consideration shown by university and School. Here, I was not just a researcher but also engaged in teaching assistant role, which helped solidify my foundational knowledge and enhance my teaching abilities through interactions with students and lecturers. Witnessing former students successfully applying to prestigious graduate schools abroad fills me with pride. Moreover, the university provided the opportunity for a three to six months research visit to the University of Liverpool, significantly broadening my academic horizons and enhancing my perspective. Furthermore, the life and psychological counseling mentors helped students like me with concerns about research and personal challenges. Regular academic poster competitions provided opportunities for reflection and improvement. It is within this supportive environment that I am my peers we were able to wholeheartedly immerse ourselves in research, resulting in fruitful outcomes in the laboratory.

道阻且长，行则将至

LONG AND DIFFICULT AS THE JOURNEY MAY BE, SUSTAINED ACTIONS WILL TAKE US TO THE DESTINATION

四年西浦博士生涯，一晃而过，也感谢始终不曾放弃的自己。无数个坚守在实验室的日子，无数个奋笔疾书的夜晚，无数个自我治愈的瞬间，都是成长的印记。心若有所向往，何惧道阻且长。希望自己能够继续保持对学术的初心、对科研的热忱，坚定前行，不负期盼，不负教诲，虽千万人吾往矣。

Four years of doctoral study at XJTLU have swiftly passed, and I am grateful for my unwavering dedication. Countless days spent in the laboratory, countless nights devoted to writing and numerous moments of self-healing have shaped my growth. With aspirations in my heart, I fear no long and arduous journey ahead. I hope to maintain my initial enthusiasm for academia, continue pursuing knowledge fervently, and move forward with determination, living up to expectations and teachings. Though the path ahead may be challenging, I am resolute in my pursuit.

春风风人，夏雨雨人。这四年间的专业学习及经历，是西浦和智能工程学院给我最宝贵的人生财富。往事堪堪亦澜澜，前路漫漫亦灿灿。借此，祝福所有相遇，天高海阔，万事胜意。祝愿母校及学院欣欣向荣，人才济济，熠熠生辉。

The specialized learning and experiences constitute the most precious wealth of my life, bestowed upon me by XJTLU and the School of Advanced Technology. Memories of the past are deep, and prospects for the future are bright. With this, I wish all whom I have encountered be successful in their endeavors. I wish prosperity and brilliance for XJTLU and SAT, with a bright and shining future.

师生故事

STORIES BETWEEN TEACHERS AND STUDENTS

苑航
HANG YUAN

从SAT启程找到自己，驶向世界

STARTING FROM SAT, FINDING ONESELF, AND SAILING TOWARDS THE WORLD

西浦是一个自由开放包容的平台。在这里，我有足够的时间和空间来探索自己喜欢的事情，无论是比赛还是科研。三年前，我通过大一下学期的专业选择进入智能工程学院（SAT）的机械电子工程（MRS）专业学习。在这个“年轻”的学院和专业里，我度过了丰富多彩的本科生活，有经验收获也有坎坷挫折。从孩子到成人再到世界公民，西浦SAT 教会我如何系好人生的一颗又一颗纽扣。

Xi'an Jiaotong-Liverpool University (XJTLU) offers a free, open, and inclusive platform. Here, I have the time and space to explore my passions, whether in competitions or research. Three years ago, I chose to enter the Mechatronics and Robotic Systems (MRS) program in the School of Advanced Technology (SAT) through the major selection process in the second semester of my freshman year. Since then, I have enjoyed a vibrant undergraduate life in this young school and program, filled with both experiences and challenges. From a child to a young adult to a global citizen, SAT has taught me how to fasten every button in the garment of life.

SAT给我的第一颗纽扣是关于“青年工程师的成长”
THE FIRST BUTTON FROM SAT, THE GROWTH OF YOUNG ENGINEERS

在一次专业分享会上，我了解到 SAT 有一支西浦自己的机器人战队“GMaster”。其间，宣传片展示的内容和我的兴趣不谋而合，在“成为一个青年工程师”理想的激励下，我很快加入了GMaster。入队之初，因为疫情出现了技术断代的情况，并且我们和高一届的学长学姐都缺乏实际的比赛经验，研发进度一度受挫。但是在学院及指导老师赵策洲教授和赵春老师的协调下，我们有了尽可能多的调试场地和专业学习机会。此外，一些相关专业的老师和已经退役的学长学姐也会在自己的闲暇时间来实验室帮助我们进行研发。而在一个晚上，我向赵教授介绍了研发情况后，他拍了拍我说：“有你们这些年轻人，我相信队伍就有希望。”在那个夜晚，我还不明白这句话意味着什么，只是把它记在心里。可没想到，后来却成了教授对我的“最后的嘱托”。

During a professional sharing session, I discovered that SAT manages a robotics team called "GMaster". The promotional video showcased content that perfectly aligned with my interests. Inspired by the goal of becoming a young engineer, I quickly joined GMaster.At first, COVID-19 had caused a technological gap, and both we and the senior students lacked actual competition experience, leading to setbacks in our development progress. However, with the coordination of the SAT and the guidance of Prof. Cezhou Zhao and Dr. Chun Zhao, we secured many testing spaces and professional learning opportunities. Additionally, professors and retired senior team members dedicated their spare time in the lab to assist us with robot development. One evening, after I briefly introduced our progress to Prof. Zhao, he patted me on the back and said: "Young people like you are the future of the team." At that moment, I didn't grasp the significance of his words; I simply remembered them. Little did I know, this would be the professor's final words of advice to me.

2021 年 RoboMaster 高校联盟赛江苏站的前一天，赵教授永远地离开了我们。次日，南京，因实战经验不足，GMaster 无缘晋级。回程的大巴上，所有人沉默不语。只是在那之后，大家来实验室的次数更多了，待的时间更久了。

On the day before the 2021 RoboMaster University League of Jiangsu Province, Prof. Zhao passed away unexpectedly. The next day, due to a lack of practical experience, GMaster did not advance in Nanjing. Everyone remained silent on the return bus. Following this event, we began coming to the lab more frequently and staying longer.

2021 年夏天，台风“烟花”登陆，在深圳春茧体育场，GMaster 以两胜一平的成绩拿下 RoboMaster 国际赛区亚军，创造了西浦队历史最好成绩。

In the summer of 2021, as Typhoon In-Fa struck, GMaster secured the runner-up position in the RoboMaster University Championship International Division at the Shenzhen Bay Sports Center, with two wins and one draw, achieving the best result in XJTLU history.

2022 年夏天，在常州，GMaster 入围东部赛区区域赛八强，进入全国三十二强，拿到 RoboMaster 全国赛入场券，再次刷新西浦队历史最好成绩。

In the summer of 2022, in Changzhou, GMaster advanced to the top eight in the RoboMaster University Championship Eastern Division. We reached the top 32 nationwide and earned a spot in the National Competition, once again setting a new record for XJTLU.

刚进入 SAT 的时候，我对于内心的理想还不够明确，但是在老师的教导、队友的鼓励和学院的支持下，我了解了我自己，找到了自己的兴趣爱好，明确了自己的责任。SAT 给我们这群年轻人提供了一个良好的生态，让青年工程师汇聚在一起追求技术的极致、践行对工程的热爱。

在 GMaster 机器人战队的故事里，一群青年工程师从零开始，一步步走向最高的全国对抗赛舞台。除了专业上的指导，SAT 在精神上对我的影响更加深远。我想，用“薪火相传”四个字来概括更为贴切。

When I first joined SAT, I was unsure about my goals. However, with the guidance of my teachers, the encouragement of my teammates, and the support of the SAT, I came to understand myself, discover my interests, and embrace responsibilities. SAT provided a healthy ecosystem where young engineers could pursue technical excellence and share a passion for engineering.

In the story of the team GMaster, a group of young engineers started from scratch and gradually advanced to the top stage of the national competition. Beyond professional guidance, the SAT has had an even more profound impact on me spiritually. I believe the phrase "pass the flame" perfectly encapsulates this experience.

SAT给我的第二颗纽扣是关于“大学生创业的尝试”
THE SECOND BUTTON FROM SAT, THE ATTEMPT OF UNIVERSITY STUDENTS TO START A BUSINESS

无论是在课上还是课后，我们一直被尽可能地给予独立的空间、决策的机会和尝试的权利。2021年的春天，我看到了西浦公众号推送的一则“创业比赛”活动，“创业”对那时的我来说是一个遥远的词，但是一直以来我热衷于尝试新鲜事物，这也是西浦所支持的。

Whether in class or outside, we have always been given independent space, decision-making opportunities, and the freedom to try. In the spring of 2021, I noticed an entrepreneurship competition activity promoted on the XJTLU official WeChat account. "Entrepreneurship" was a strange concept for me at that time, but I have always been keen on trying new things, which XJTLU also supports.

作为一个工科生，我希望从“接地气”的工程技术入手来开展我的第一次创业尝试。从高中以来，我对于 3D 打印都有着浓厚的兴趣，在大学时又正好遇到国产桌面级 3D 打印机开始在市场推广。于是，我提出了“校园 3D 打印”的想法。但是，我和团队都缺乏相关的技术转化经验。在 SAT 定期举办的多个科研分享会和讲座中，我认识了许多专业的老师。在听完我的想法和诉求后，老师们都非常支持，也帮我从学院寻求到一些资金支持，以帮助我完成初期演示。

As an engineering student, I aimed to initiate my first entrepreneurial attempt from a practical engineering technology perspective. Since high school, I have been deeply interested in 3D printing, and during university, domestic desktop 3D printers began to be marketed. Thus, I proposed the idea of campus 3D printing. However, my team and I lacked experience in technology transfer. Through several scientific research sharing sessions and lectures regularly held by SAT, I connected with many professional teachers. Upon hearing my ideas and needs, the teachers were very supportive and helped secure financial backing from SAT to complete the initial demonstration.

在路演过程中，我一直都很放松，并没有把这次“创业”当成是一个庞大的项目，而当它是一次重要的团队磨合和尝试新事物的机会。最终，我们成了所有参赛项目中完全由大一学生组成并且第一次参加就获得全校第一的团队，次年蝉联冠军，并且在常州市政府的支持下成立了第一家公司。

During the roadshow process, I remained relaxed and did not view this "entrepreneurship" as a daunting project, but rather a significant opportunity for team cohesion and exploration. Finally, we emerged as the top-ranked team among all participating projects, entirely composed of freshmen participating for the first time. The following year, we successfully defended the championship. With support from the Changzhou government, we also established our first company.

在创业的故事里，一群志同道合的西浦人从尝试开始，一步步成为一个坚实的团队。SAT 为我们提供了一个“打磨想法的工坊”，教会我如何将视野拓展到技术本身之外，培养跨学科领导力以及主动思考的能力。创新精神的传递和平台的搭建，让高校这个“象牙塔”离社会更近了一些，让我在不确定的世界里勇敢寻路。

In the entrepreneurial journey, a group of like-minded XJTLUers started with an attempt and gradually formed a cohesive team. SAT provided a workshop for refining ideas, teaching me to expand my horizons beyond technology alone, cultivate interdisciplinary leadership, and develop proactive thinking abilities. The transmission of innovative spirit and the establishment of platforms bridge universities closer to society, empowering me to navigate confidently in an uncertain world and find my path.

SAT给我的第三颗纽扣是关于"研究导向型的科研"
The third button from SAT, research-oriented research

将电子引入传统的机械工程——MRS，这个刚刚开设三年的“年轻”专业，相比那些有着几百人的专业，刚开始只有区区几十人，但是这也形成了小班化的教学模式，能够与系里专业老师有更多的接触机会。

Introducing electronics into traditional mechanical engineering—MRS, a young program established just three years ago. Compared to programs with hundreds of students, MRS initially had only a few dozen students, fostering a small-class teaching model and providing more opportunities to interact closely with departmental teachers.

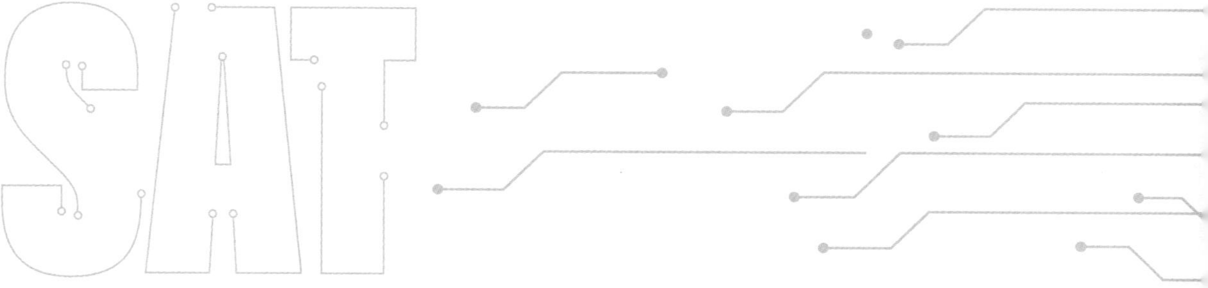

2021 年夏天，通过本科生暑期科研项目（SURF），我加入了陈敏老师和张权老师的团队进行机器人相关项目研究。虽然我还是本科生，但是 SAT 依然为我提供了国际化的资源和经验，从提出想法到动手实践再到展示表达，培养了我解决问题的科研能力。在此期间，我的学习开始向主动性的、研究性的学习转变。张老师发现了我对交叉学科研究的兴趣，于是将我推荐给了宋鹏飞老师从事微流控方面的研究工作。

在宋老师的指导下，我的研究项目总体围绕纸基微流控生物传感展开。即使在疫情居家期间，宋老师仍然支持并指导我进行学术训练，为我介绍和讲解他博士期间在微流控分选秀丽隐杆线虫方面的工作。随着研究的深入，我越来越清楚前进的目标——申请直博。

In the summer of 2021, I participated in the Undergraduate Summer Research Fellowship (SURF) and joined Dr. Min Chen and Dr. Quan Zhang's team for a robotics-related project. Despite being an undergraduate student, the SAT still provided me with access to international resources and experiences. From proposing ideas to hands-on implementation and presentation, SAT cultivated my research ability to solve problems actively. During this period, I began to transition towards active and research-oriented learning. Recognizing my interest in interdisciplinary research, Dr. Zhang recommended me to Dr. Pengfei Song to work on microfluidics.

Under Dr. Song's guidance, my research project focused on paper-based microfluidics for biosensing. Despite the challenges posed by COVID-19, Dr. Song continued to support and guide me in academic training, introducing and explaining his doctoral work on microfluidic-assisted C. elegans sorting. As my research deepened, I became increasingly focused on my goal—to apply for a direct Ph.D. program.

宋老师及 SAT 的其他老师们知道我的想法后，时常关心我遇到的学术难题并且尽可能地为我提供专业训练的机会，无论是科研交流还是参观学习。在条件允许的情况下，学院为本科生尽可能地提供科研资金、设备和场地，鼓励参加国际交流。在 SAT 的支持下，我不仅参加了在澳大利亚悉尼举办的生物医学工程盛会 IEEE EMBC，还以工科学生的身份深入人文社科和教育领域，真正地了解不同学科的工作方式。从学生的角度参与到教学创新中去，这正是西浦提倡的“研究导向和兴趣驱动的学习”。最终，我收到了多个全奖直博通知书，将进入美国密歇根州立大学生物医学工程专业学习，攻读博士学位。

After Dr. Song and other SAT teachers learned about my aspirations, they frequently supported me by addressing my academic challenges and providing opportunities for professional training, including research exchanges and study visits. Within the allowed conditions, the SAT generously provided research funding, equipment, and facilities for undergraduate students, encouraging me to participate in international exchanges. With the support of SAT, I attended the Annual International Conference of the IEEE Engineering in Medicine & Biology Conference (EMBC'2023) held in Sydney, Australia. Additionally, I explored humanities, social sciences, and education as an engineering student, gaining insights into diverse disciplines. Engaging in teaching innovation from a student's perspective aligns with XJTLU's emphasis on research-oriented and interest-driven learning. Ultimately, I received full-scholarship offers for direct Ph.D. programs and will pursue a doctoral degree in Biomedical Engineering at Michigan State University.

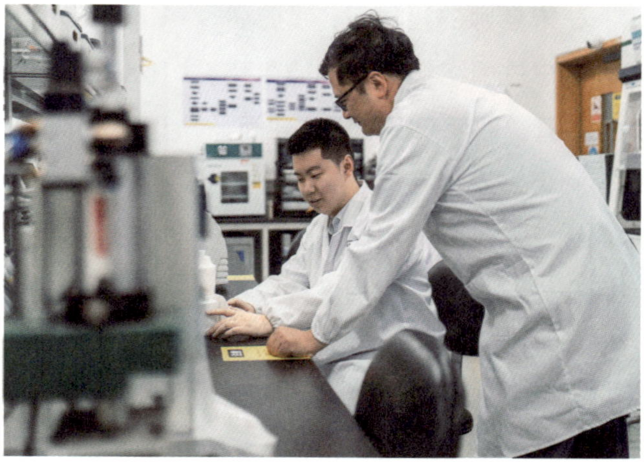

在全奖直博的故事里，与盲目或被动的学习抗争，一步步将对于交叉学科的兴趣和动力从机械电子工程转到生物医学工程。SAT 提供了一个“搭建未来事业的舞台”，支持我们每一个自主的、正向的、独立的决定，SAT 以其宽阔的国际视野让我们在学习旅程中具有国际竞争力。

我们从 SAT 启程，接受不确定性的洗礼，从危机中挖掘机会，从尝试中寻找自己，最终驶向世界。正如校训“博学明道，笃行任事”所言，终身学习，恭谨谦卑，是西浦人永远的追求。

In the journey towards receiving full-scholarship offers for direct Ph.D. programs, I moved away from blind or passive learning, gradually shifting my interest and motivation from mechatronics to biomedical engineering. SAT provided a stage for building future careers, supporting our autonomous, positive, and independent decisions. With its broad international perspective, SAT made us globally competitive in our learning journey.

We set out from SAT, embracing the baptism of uncertainty, uncovering opportunities from crises, discovering ourselves through attempts, and ultimately sailing toward the world. As XJTLU's motto "Light and Wings" suggests, lifelong learning, humility, and diligence are the eternal pursuits of XJTLUers.

展望未来
LOOKING TO THE FUTURE

五载春秋，恍如白驹过隙，但在这飞逝的时光里，却铭刻下了难以磨灭的印记。这五年，是我们用智慧和汗水共同浇灌的五年，是学院从稚嫩走向成熟的五年。

我常常回首过去，沉思学院的成长是否与我们最初的梦想相吻合。正如人不能忘记初心，学院也不能忘记它为何而诞生。我们在这片热土上辛勤耕耘，用科研的火花点燃智慧的灯塔，让创新的种子在这片土地上生根发芽，茁壮成长。

在这里，我们共同见证了无数的奇迹与突破。从无到有，从未知到已知，从现有到创新，每一步都凝聚着我们的汗水和智慧。当然，我们也经历了离别，但那些离去的人们，我们终将缅怀，他们的精神、他们的智慧、他们的工作态度，都将成为我们未来道路上的宝贵财富。

Five years have elapsed in the blink of an eye, yet within this fleeting time, enduring impressions have been made. These five years represent the culmination of our collective wisdom and hard work, signifying the evolution of the School from its inception to maturity.

I often reflect, contemplating on whether the School' s progress aligns with our original aspirations. Just as individuals should not forget their initial intents, the School too must not lose sight of its initial purpose. We have laboured diligently on this fertile ground, kindling the flame of wisdom with sparks of scientific research, and nurturing the seeds of innovation to take root, flourish, and thrive in this environment.

Here, we have collectively borne witness to countless wonders and advancements. From non-existence to existence, from the unknown to the known, from conventional to innovative, each step embodies our hard work and wisdom. Naturally, we have also bid farewell to some, but those who have departed will always hold a special place in our hearts. Their spirit, wisdom, and work ethic will continue to be cherished assets on our journey forward.

我深爱着这个学院、这个充满活力和希望的大家庭。作为这个大家庭的家长，我渴望为大家创造一个温馨、舒适的工作环境，让每一个人都能在这里快乐地工作、快乐地生活、快乐地分享。我期待着未来，期待着更多志同道合的人们加入我们的行列，共同为学院的明天添砖加瓦。

I hold a deep affection for this School, this vivacious and optimistic family. As the guardian of this extended family, I aspire to create a warm and comfortable working environment for all, allowing each individual to work, live, and find joy here. I eagerly anticipate the future, looking forward to welcoming more like-minded individuals to our community, collectively contributing to the School's future.

下一个五年，我们将继续携手前行，共同迎接更多的挑战和机遇。当你在校园里看到我的头发又愈发花白，就知道我们是有多努力了。我相信，只要我们齐心协力、锐意进取，学院的明天一定会更加辉煌灿烂。

Over the next five years, we will persevere together, embracing further challenges and opportunities. When you see my hair turning even whiter on campus, you will recognize the extent of our dedication. I firmly believe that as long as we stand united and press forward, the School's tomorrow will undoubtedly be even more magnificent and splendid.

在这值得纪念的日子里，我衷心祝愿智能工程学院五周年生日快乐！愿它如同初升的太阳，永远充满活力和希望；愿它的未来更加美好，更加辉煌！

On this special anniversary, I wholeheartedly extend my best wishes to the School of Advanced Technology on its happy 5th anniversary! May it remain as vibrant and optimistic as the rising sun, and may its future be even brighter and more magnificent!

“他们说……”——教职工

孙捷
Jie Sun

在过去五年中，SAT 已发展成为教育领域的卓越典范，营造出一个让学生在智力和个性方面蓬勃发展的培养环境。衷心感谢我们敬业的教师、员工、学生和支持我们的家长，他们的坚定承诺和热情是成功的基石。我们共同建立了一个以好奇心、创新和诚信为价值观的充满活力的社区。

Over the past five years, SAT has blossomed into a beacon of excellence in education, fostering a nurturing environment where students thrive intellectually and personally. We extend our heartfelt gratitude to our dedicated faculty, staff, students, and supportive parents whose unwavering commitment and passion have been the cornerstone of our success. Together, we have cultivated a vibrant community grounded in the values of curiosity, innovation, and integrity.

能够在博士一毕业就加入智能工程学院，我感到非常幸运。这里的支持与帮助对我的成长起到了至关重要的作用。我非常感激能够与如此敬业的同事们一同学习和成长。让我们共同庆祝之前取得的成绩，也预祝学院未来继续取得更大的成功！

I feel incredibly fortunate to have joined such a nurturing school right after Ph.D. graduating. The supportive environment here has been instrumental in shaping my professional journey. I am grateful for the opportunities to learn and grow alongside such dedicated colleagues and leaders. Here's to celebrating our achievements and looking forward to a future filled with continued success and collaboration!

宋鹏飞
Pengfei Song

卜庆雷
Qinglei Bu

祝贺 SAT 五周年这一重要里程碑的到来，它体现了奉献、决心、追求知识和创新的价值观。愿 SAT 在未来的岁月里，培育出更多优秀的创新者，取得创新性的发现和持久的成功。

Congratulations on reaching this significant milestone, the fifth anniversary of the SAT. It embodies the values of dedication, determination, and the pursuit of knowledge and innovation. May the years ahead be distinguished by the inspiration of future innovators, innovative discoveries, and enduring success.

五周年快乐！合并两个系而成立的 SAT 是真正的 1+1 大于 2。作为我们学院的一分子我很自豪，也很享受这段旅程。祝贺我们取得了如此难以置信的里程碑。我迫不及待地想知道我们学院的美好未来！

Happy 5th Anniversary!It is really 1+1 >2 by merging two departments to form SAT. Congratulations on reaching this an incredible milestone. I'm excited to see what the future holds for us.

王秋锋
Qiufeng Wang

“他们说……”——教职工

弹指一挥间，智能工程学院已走过五个春秋。风雨兼程，不忘初心再出发。这五年，是筚路蓝缕奠基立业的五年，是创造辉煌开辟未来的五年。愿学院的明天更加灿烂，教育之花常开不败，培养出更多栋梁之才。愿学院的每一步都踏实而坚定，走向更加辉煌的未来。

Over the past five years, SAT has swiftly evolved, navigating both challenges and milestones with steadfast commitment. As we look ahead, I wish for our school to continue to flourish its educational endeavors blossoming steadily, cultivating talents who will become pillars of the community and a source of enduring pride. May each step SAT take be strong and decisive, leading us toward a more radiant future.

武芳宇
Fangyu Wu

在 SAT 工作的每一天都是愉快的。我为能够同 SAT 一起庆祝五周年院庆感到荣幸。五年是 SAT 发展的一个重要里程碑。我希望 SAT 在下一个五年能够更加辉煌！

It is alway enjoyable working as a member of SAT. I am honoured as a SAT member for the celebration of the five year anniversary. Five years is an important milestone that remarks the progress had been made. I wish SAT a better future in the next five years.

李圣辰
Shengchen Li

王炤
Zhao Wang

在学院成立五周年之际，祝我们的学院在未来能够蓬勃发展，教学科研取得更大成就，培养出更多优秀人才，为社会贡献更多智慧与力量。让我们携手努力，共同书写美好的未来！

On the 5th anniversary of SAT, I wish for our school to continue thriving, achieving greater success in teaching and research, and nurturing more outstanding students who will contribute wisdom and strength to society. Let us work together to create a bright future!

祝福 SAT 承载学生和老师们的梦想砥砺前行、扬帆远航。

Wish the SAT family all the smoothness and prosperity.

余丽敏
Limin Yu

“他们说……” —— 教职工

智能工程学院五周年快乐！祝愿学院在未来的日子里再创辉煌，为学生创造更加美好的学习环境，让他们充分发挥潜力。愿下一个五年带来更多成就和里程碑。

Congratulations to SAT on your five-year anniversary! I wish you continued success in fostering a vibrant learning community and empowering students to reach their full potential. May the next five years bring even greater achievements and milestones.

樊文晙
Wenjun Fan

五年的风雨同舟，我们共同见证了学院的发展和成功。让我们整装再出发，共同谱写新的辉煌篇章。

Five years of standing together, regardless of hardships, we have witnessed the development and success of the SAT. Let us embark on a new journey together to create a new brilliant chapter.

朱晓辉
Xiaohui Zhu

很高兴能见证学院的五周年生日。SAT 不仅是一座学习的殿堂，更是一个温暖的港湾。期待学院培养出更多优秀的学子，继续为社会的发展贡献力量。

I am so excited to witness the 5th Anniversary of the School. SAT is not only a temple of learning but also a warm harbor. Looking forward to the school nurturing more outstanding students and contributing to the development of society.

项南
Nan Xiang

衷心祝愿 SAT：在未来的人工智能十年好上加好，持续保持五星级的教育科研与服务，并能跻身全球五十名校。

All the best wishes to SAT:
moving into the AI era to continue to excel in education, research and service to the community to achieve five-star quality amongst top fifty world ranking in the next ten years.

关圣威
Steven Guan

“他们说……”——教职工

期望 SAT 在中国学术界具有更加显著的影响力和声誉。期望在未来五年，SAT 的电气工程专业可以闯入中国大学前 100 强。期望我们基于人工智能技术的电力系统安全领域的研究，在不远的将来能获得丰硕的成果。

Hope SAT could have more impacts and reputations in Chinese academic circles. Hope Electrical Engineering of SAT could be ranked in top 100 in Chinese Universities in the coming five years. Hope our research about power system security by AI technologies could be more fruitful in the near future.

薛飞
Fei Xue

祝 SAT 五周年快乐！身为 SAT 的一员，能在这个多元文化交融的环境中探索创新和学术发展我深感荣幸。我衷心祝愿学院能够持续稳步发展，并为来自不同背景的学生提供一个广阔的发展平台，使其绽放最高潜力之光彩。

Happy Five-Year Anniversary to the School of Advanced Technology! As a staff member, I deeply appreciate our diverse cultural environment, which has been crucial to our innovation and academic excellence. May our school continue to thrive, inspiring and empowering students from all backgrounds to reach their highest potential.

吴烨
Ye Wu

陈晓阳
Xiaoyang Chen

智能工程学院五周年生日快乐！今年也是我加入 SAT 的第三年，感恩一路走来相遇的大家。展望未来，愿学院继续乘风破浪，勇往直前，智能启航，未来已来。

Happy 5th birthday to SAT! This is my third year in SAT, and I'm thankful for all the people I've met along the way. Looking to the future, may the School continue to ride the waves, Gunbuster, smart sailing, the future has come.

“他们说……”——学生

愿智能工程学院在未来的岁月里，继续培养出更多具有创新精神和实践能力的人才，引领科技教育的潮流。五周年之际，愿学院的学术成就与社会影响力更上一层楼，成为培养未来科技领袖的摇篮。

May the SAT continue to cultivate more talents with innovative spirit and practical abilities in the years to come, leading the trend of technological education. On the occasion of its fifth anniversary, may the School's academic achievements and social influence reach new heights, becoming a cradle for nurturing future technology leaders.

王诗雯
Shiwen Wang

恭喜 SAT 迎来五周年！感谢每一位师生对 SAT 的辛勤付出与无私奉献！在未来的日子里，愿 SAT 继续勇攀高峰，培养更多杰出人才，共创美好明天！

Congratulations on the 5th anniversary of SAT! Thanks to every teacher, staff and student for their hard work and selfless dedication to SAT! In the coming days, may SAT continue to reach new heights, train more outgoing talents, and create a better tomorrow!

路畅
Chang Lu

于阔
Kuo Yu

技术够硬，身体够棒，学院够强！

Skill on point, body like a rock, school top-notch !

祝愿 SAT 五周年生日快乐，未来更加辉煌灿烂，培养更多杰出人才！

May SAT continue to thrive and shine, nurturing exceptional talents for the future!

范世睿
Shirui Fan

岑昕
Xin Cen

五年时间见证了 SAT 从成立到硕果累累。众多优秀的教职人员、学生和校友都在 SAT 留下了努力的瞬间。祝愿 SAT 在以后的每个五年都能不断进步发展。

SAT achieved a lot in the past five years. Many talented staff, students and alumni have hard-working moments at SAT. Best wishes to SAT for continued progress and growth in each of the five years to come!

“他们说……”——学生

智能工程学院五周年快乐！感谢学院这五年来为学生提供的知识与机会。同时也非常怀念在学院的时光，希望SAT 在未来的岁月中继续培养出具有创新精神和实践能力的学生！

Happy 5th anniversary of SAT! I would like to thank the school for providing students with knowledge and opportunities. At the same time, hope SAT continue to train innovative and experimental students in the future!

王敏泽
Minze Wang

王纬诺
Weinuo Wang

五载风雨，智能工程学院铸就辉煌。愿未来岁月，学院科研创新更上层楼，学子们前程似锦，共筑科技强国梦！

Five years of challenges and growth, the SAT has flourished. May it continue to soar in research and education, empowering its students to create a brighter technological future for our nation!

祝贺智能工程学院成立五周年！感谢学院给我提供了宝贵的学习机会，我在这里留下了很多难忘的回忆。希望学院以后越办越好！

Congratulations on the fifth anniversary of SAT! Thank you for providing me with valuable learning opportunities and unforgettable memories. I hope the school continues to thrive in the future!

杨帆
Fan Yang

吴世强
Shiqiang Wu

祝贺智能工程学院成立五周年！作为一名大四即将毕业的学生，能够见证学院的蓬勃发展我深感荣幸。五年来，学院在学术研究、科技创新和人才培养方面取得了卓越的成就。我衷心祝愿学院在未来的岁月里继续引领科技前沿，培养更多具有创新精神和实践能力的专业人才，创造更加辉煌的明天！

Congratulations on the 5th anniversary of SAT! As a senior student about to graduate, I feel deeply honored to witness the vigorous development of School. Over the past five years, School has made outstanding achievements in academic research, scientific and technological innovation and personnel training. I sincerely hope that School will continue to lead the forefront of science and technology in the coming years, train more professionals with innovative spirit and practical ability, and create a more brilliant tomorrow!

希望 SAT 保持那一份热爱奔向下一场山海，之后的学习仍有意义又自在。

Hoping that SAT can keep the love and rush to the future, and the learning after that is still meaningful and comfortable.

赵子轩
Zixuan Zhao

“他们说……”——学生

祝智能工程学院蒸蒸日上！五年来，学院目睹了学生们的成长，也见证了自身的蜕变。长风破浪会有时，直挂云帆济沧海。尽管仍显稚嫩，但我坚信，在未来的岁月里，大家能携手共进，用我们的汗水与成就书写学院的辉煌历史与深厚底蕴。

Wishing the School of Advanced Technology continued success! Over the past five years, School has witnessed the growth of its students and its own transformation. "There will be times when the wind and waves will break, and the sail will be hung straight to cross the sea." Though still young, I firmly believe that in the years to come, we will join hands and, with our sweat and achievements, write the glorious history and rich heritage of the school.

许心宇
Xinyu Xu

感谢这四年学院给予我们最专业的指导和最自由的学习环境，让我们在知识的海洋中遨游。你们的支持和鼓励铸就了我们今天的成长。祝学院五周年生日快乐，未来更加辉煌，培养出更多卓越的人才！

Dear SAT, thank you for the past four years of providing us with the most professional guidance and the freest learning environment, allowing us to explore the ocean of knowledge. Your support and encouragement have shaped our growth today. Happy 5th anniversary to SAT! May it continue to thrive and cultivate more outstanding talents!

刘怡凡
Yifan Liu

五载春秋，智慧绽放。作为智能工程学院毕业的学生，学院见证了我的成长和蜕变。愿学院蒸蒸日上、蓬勃发展，培养出更多引领时代的精英人才！

Five years of spring and autumn, wisdom blossoms.SAT has witnessed my growth and transformation. I wish my school continue to prosper and flourish, nurturing more elite talents to lead the times!

翟传欣
Chuanxin Zhai